THE ESSENTIAL POETS

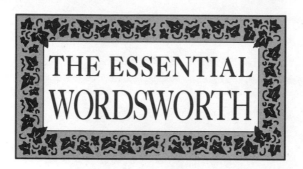

THE ESSENTIAL
WORDSWORTH

William Wordsworth

BORN   7 APRIL 1770
DIED   23 APRIL 1850

THE ESSENTIAL
WORDSWORTH

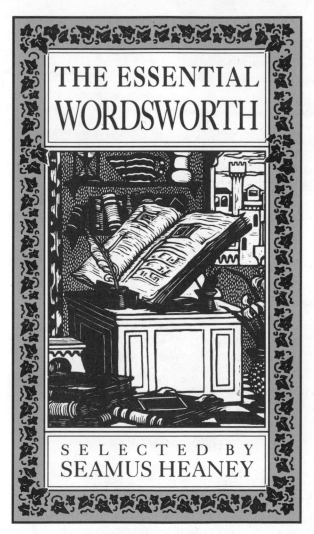

SELECTED BY
SEAMUS HEANEY

GALAHAD BOOKS
NEW YORK

Published in 1993 by Galahad Books
A division of Budget Book Service, Inc.
386 Park Avenue South
New York, NY 10016
Galahad Books is a registered trademark
of Budget Book Service, Inc.

This edition published by arrangement with The Ecco Press

Library of Congress Catalog Card Number: 88-4260
ISBN: 0-88365-835-6

Original design by Reg Perry
Additional art and design for this edition by Cindy LaBreacht

Portrait "William Wordsworth at the Age of 36" by
Henry Edridge. Copyright by the Trustees of Dove Cottage.
Courtesy of The Wordsworth Trust, Dove Cottage, Grasmere.

Printed in the United States of America.

For Sean B. O'Kelly

 CONTENTS

INTRODUCTION BY SEAMUS HEANEY   3

POEMS   15

Written in Very Early Youth   15

The Ruined Cottage   15

Animal Tranquillity and Decay   32

Fragment: Yet once again   32

Fragments from the Alfoxden Notebook (1)   33

To My Sister   34

Goody Blake and Harry Gill   36

Lines Written in Early Spring   40

Expostulation and Reply   41

The Tables Turned   42

Lines Composed a Few Miles above Tintern Abbey . . .   44

There Was a Boy   49

A slumber did my spirit seal   50

She dwelt among the untrodden ways   50

Strange fits of passion have I known   51

Nutting   52

Lucy Gray; or, Solitude   54

Fragment: Redundance   56

Three years she grew in sun and shower   57

A narrow girdle of rough stones and crags   58

Michael: A Pastoral Poem   61

from *Preface to* Lyrical Ballads, with Pastoral   76
and Other Poems *(1802)*

The Two-Part Prelude   87

from *The Prelude (1805)*   117
Book IV. Summer Vacation, lines 363–504.
Book VI. Cambridge and the Alps, lines 332–425.
Book IX. Residence in France, lines 217–346; lines 510–542.
Book X. Residence in France, lines 230–275; lines 865–941.
Book XIII. Conclusion, lines 1–119.

I travelled among unknown men   137

To the Cuckoo   137

My heart leaps up when I behold   139

Ode: Intimations of Immortality   139
from Recollections of Early Childhood

Resolution and Independence   146

Travelling   152

1801   152

Great men have been among us; hands that penned   153

Personal Talk   153

The world is too much with us; late and soon   154

To the Memory of Raisley Calvert   154

With Ships the sea was sprinkled far and nigh   155

Composed Upon Westminster Bridge, September 3, 1802   155

Composed near Calais, on the Road   156
Leading to Ardres, August 7, 1802

It is a beauteous evening, calm and free   156

To Toussaint l'Ouverture   157

Calais, August 15, 1802   157

September, 1802. Near Dover   158

London, 1802   158

Written in London, September, 1802   159

October, 1803   159

Yarrow Unvisited   160

The Small Celandine   162

I wandered lonely as a cloud   163

French Revolution As It Appeared   164
to Enthusiasts at Its Commencement

The Simplon Pass   166

Elegiac Stanzas Suggested by a Picture of Peele Castle,   166
in a Storm, Painted by Sir George Beaumont

Stepping Westward   169

The Solitary Reaper   170

Thought of a Briton on the Subjugation of Switzerland   171

Though narrow be that old Man's cares, and near   172

Composed by the Side of Grasmere Lake   172

Surprised by joy—impatient as the Wind   173

Lines   173
from *The River Duddon*   174
XXXIV After-Thought
Extempore Effusion upon the Death of James Hogg   175
ABOUT THE EDITOR   177

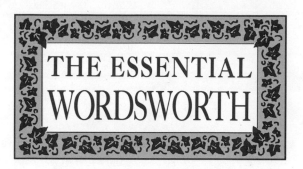

THE ESSENTIAL
WORDSWORTH

 INTRODUCTION

As a child, William Wordsworth imagined he heard the moorlands breathing on his neck. He rowed in panic as a cliff pursued him across moonlit water, saw a drowned man rise out of Esthwaite Lake "Bolt upright . . . with his ghastly face," and once, as a five-year-old lost in the hills east of Penrith Beacon, found himself beside a gibbet post believed to mark the scene of a murder and an execution. Letters had been cut into the turf at the foot of the post—T.P.M., meaning "Thomas Parker Murdered"—and although the body of the gibbeted murderer had disappeared, the place and its associations were enough to send the child fleeing in terror to the beacon summit.

Every childhood has its share of correspondingly uncanny moments. Nowadays, however, in post-Freudian, post-Jungian, if not post-Romantic conditions, it is easy to underestimate the originality and confidence of a writer who came to consciousness in Dr. Johnson's supremely adult eighteenth century and who yet managed to force a way through literary convention and established modes of feeling to find in such moments not only the source of his emotional being, but the clue to his fulfilled identity.

By his late twenties, Wordsworth knew this one big truth and during the next ten years he kept developing its implications with intense excitement, industry, and concentration. During this period, he also elaborated a necessary personal idiom: "nature" and "imagination" are not words that belong exclusively to a Wordsworthian discourse, yet they arise insistently and inevitably when we consider this poet whose achievement, since Milton's, is the most securely founded in the canon

of native English poetry. He is an indispensable figure in the evolution of modern writing, a finder and keeper of the self-as-subject, a theorist and apologist whose Preface to *Lyrical Ballads* (1802) remains definitive.

Wordsworth's power over us stems from the manifest strength of his efforts to integrate several strenuous and potentially contradictory efforts. More than a century before Yeats imposed upon himself the order to hammer his thoughts into unity, Wordsworth was fulfilling it with resolute intent. Indeed, it is not until Yeats that we encounter another poet in whom emotional susceptibility, intellectual force, psychological acuteness, political awareness, artistic self-knowledge, and bardic representativeness are so truly and responsibly combined. (William Blake also comes to mind, but he does not possess—indeed he would have disdained—the "representativeness.")

Take, for example, a poem like "Resolution and Independence." Democratic, even republican, in its characteristic eye-level encounter with the outcast, and in its curiosity about his economic survival. Visionary in its presentation of the old man transfigured by the moment of epiphany. Philosophic in its retrieval of the stance of wisdom out of the experience of wonder. Cathartic in the forthrightness of its self-analysis. Masterful in its handling of the Spenserian stanza, a mastery not come by without many previous efforts in the form. Salutary—not just picturesque—in its evocation of landscape and weather, inciting us to perceive connections between the leech-gatherer's ascetic majesty and the austere setting of moorland, cloud, and pool. In a word, Wordsworthian.

Furthermore, "Resolution and Independence" exemplifies the kind of revolutionary poem Wordsworth envisaged in the Preface. It takes its origin from "emotion recollected in tranquillity"; that emotion is contemplated until "by a species of reaction the tranquillity gradually disappears, and an emotion, kindred to that which was before the subject of contemplation, is gradually produced and does actually exist in the mind." What happens also in the new poetry (again, these are the terms

of the Preface) is that a common incident is viewed under a certain "colouring of imagination"; ordinary things are presented to the mind in an unusual way and made interesting by the poet's capacity to trace in them, "truly though not ostentatiously, the primary laws of our nature."

Faced with the almost geological sobriety of works like "Tintern Abbey," "Michael," "The Ruined Cottage," and the celebrated "spots of time" in *The Prelude,* one tends to forget that they are the work of a young man. These poems, which enabled Wordsworth to speak with such authority—not just about the creative process but about the attributes of a poetry adequate to contemporary conditions—were written while he was still in his twenties. Yet the note is sure, the desire to impress absent, and the poems thoroughly absorbed in their own unglamorous necessities.

One of the reasons why Wordsworth's poems communicate such an impression of wholeness and depth is that they arrived as the hard-earned reward of resolved crisis. The steady emotional keel beneath them has known tempestuous conditions. As we shall see, they are songs of a man who has come through, one in whom William Hazlitt noted "a worn pressure of thought about his temples, a fire in the eye . . . an intense, high narrow forehead, a Roman nose, cheeks furrowed with deep purpose and feelings." That was in 1795, when the poet had almost weathered the storm and was lingering in the south of England, in the vernal clearings of Racedown in Dorset. There, somewhat prematurely on the chronological scale, but with perfect timing on the psychological one, he was about to undertake the Dantesque, midlife journey in memory, back through the dark wood.

At this auspicious moment, his Beatrice was no ethereal sublimation but his volatile and highly intelligent sister, Dorothy. His Virgil was the guiding, philosophic poet Samuel Taylor Coleridge, who, like Dante's authoritative mentor, also sent abroad "a wide river of

speech." These two were the guardians not just of Wordsworth's well-being but also of his moral being, encouragers of his poetic ambition and daily companions of his by now surely focused life. During the great creative decade that was now beginning, they functioned as auxiliary powers within his psyche for, like everyone else, a poet is extended and animated by the capacities and expectations of his friends. Coleridge's intellectual and hortatory disposition ensured that the level of aspiration stayed very high, while Dorothy's unmediated enjoyment of the given moment, indoors and out, kept her brother dramatically in touch with his own project—which was to cherish as a gift and a natural education every significant experience that occurs in the ordinary run of a lifetime.

Alfoxden, Grasmere: another "essential" selection could be made from the pages of the journals Dorothy Wordsworth kept in these places. The Racedown period had begun in September 1795, when William, freed by a legacy from his friend Raisley Calvert, could enter upon a more self-directed and withdrawn life. Then, in order to be nearer to Coleridge, who was living at Nether Stowey in Dorset, the Wordsworths moved to Alfoxden where they spent over a year in residence, at the end of which time the poets published the 1798 edition of *Lyrical Ballads,* the volume of poetry that initiates the modern enterprise. There followed a trip to Germany during which William wrote some of his most oneiric lyrics, including several "Lucy" poems, and the first draft of his autobiographical masterpiece, *The Prelude,* in the form we know now (thanks to the researches of Jonathan Wordsworth) as "The Two-Part Prelude." Finally, the truly Wordsworthian realms were occupied when the poet and his sister settled in the English Lake District, at Dove Cottage in Grasmere, at the end of 1799.

When they moved out in 1808, *The Prelude* existed as a major poem in thirteen books, William had married Mary Hutchinson and was already the father of four children, the *Lyrical Ballads* had reached a

fourth edition, a two-volume collected edition of his poems had appeared in 1807, and, all in all, the work of "the essential Wordsworth" was mostly completed.

In 1813, he would move to the stateliest of his addresses, Rydal Mount, a large, not uncomplacent house between Grasmere and Ambleside, where he and his family (still accompanied by Dorothy) lived until his death in 1850. That the poet suffered personal losses in his prime—a son and a daughter, Thomas and Catharine, died in 1812—and that his final years were darkened by Dorothy's mental breakdown and the death of another daughter, Dora, in 1847, has had little effect in lessening the general impression that as the years proceeded Wordsworth became more an institution than an individual. It is an impression not inconsistent with the sonorous expatiation of his later poetry nor with the roll call of his offices and associations—friend of the aristocracy, Distributor of Stamps for Westmoreland, Poet Laureate. He had lost the path that should have kept leading more confidently and deeply inward; still vivid as an intelligence, nationally celebrated, domestically fortified, he ended up industriously but for the most part unrewardingly marking time as a poet.

Although Wordsworth, more than any writer before him, established how truly "the child is father of the man," it was not the grand old man of Rydal Mount who was fathered by the infant born to John and Ann Wordsworth in April 1770, in Cockermouth in Cumberland. If we look for the offspring of that soon-to-be-orphaned creature being nursed in earshot of the River Derwent, we shall find him in the twenty-eight-year-old poet listening in to himself in the covert of his poetic being. The reflexiveness of the opening lines of the first *Prelude* manuscript is both typical and bemused: Wordsworth is wide awake, entering the thicket of himself like a readied hunter, as capable of deeply receptive stillness as of silent, almost erotic foragings, forward and inward:

> *Was it for this*
> *That one, the fairest of all rivers, loved*
> *To blend his murmurs with my nurse's song,*
> *And from his alder shades and rocky falls,*
> *And from his fords and shallows, sent a voice*
> *That flowed along my dreams? For this didst thou,*
> *O Derwent, travelling over the green plains*
> *Near my 'sweet birthplace', didst thou, beauteous stream,*
> *Make ceaseless music through the night and day,*
> *Which with its steady cadence tempering*
> *Our human waywardness, composed my thoughts*
> *To more than infant softness, giving me*
> *Among the fretful dwellings of mankind*
> *A knowledge, a dim earnest, of the calm*
> *Which nature breathes among the fields and groves?*
> *Beloved Derwent, fairest of all streams,*
> *Was it for this that I, a four years' child,*
> *A naked boy, among thy silent pools*
> *Made one long bathing of a summer's day,*
> *Basked in the sun, or plunged into thy streams,*
> *Alternate, all a summer's day, or coursed*
> *Over the sandy fields, and dashed the flowers*
> *Of yellow grunsel; or, when crag and hill,*
> *The woods, and distant Skiddaw's lofty height,*
> *Were bronzed with a deep radiance, stood*
> *A naked savage in the thunder-shower?*

Here we are immediately in the presence of much that is especially characteristic of Wordsworth's verse: its fluvial procedures, its murmur that does not preclude declarativeness, its onwardness that does not preclude sidewinding. It is necessary to concentrate attention on the project of his syntax, but it is also essential to allow the sensation that emanates from that undersong of narcotic vowels and pliant consonants to take possession of the ear; or, to express it in terms of bagpipe music,

to let the drone of the manner count for as much as the chanters of the meaning.

Not unexpectedly, this double requirement of surrender and vigilance is symptomatic of a double necessity which is to some extent the theme of Wordsworth's poetry but which enters it at a level even more fundamental than the thematic. I am thinking of contradictory allegiances which his work displays to the numinous and to the matter-of-fact, his conflicting awarenesses of a necessity to attend to "the calm that nature breathes" and a responsibility to confront the grievous facts of "what man has made of man," his double bind between politics and transcendence, morality and mysticism, suffering and song.

Wordsworth's crisis of the mid-1790s—we may think of it as a kind of nervous breakdown—was brought on by his attempt to live honestly by the divergent imperatives which all of these recognitions entailed. Behind him lay a childhood and schooltime of salubrious and enlarging experiences around Hawkstead, in the mountains of his native Cumberland. He had grown up visited by swimming sensations of immensity, sensing communion with a reality that began where the dominion of his senses ended, and he was therefore naturally inclined to accept the universe as a mansion of spirit rather than a congeries of matter. He also grew up in a rural society where the egalitarian spirit prevailed and the natural man behaved with reticence and fortitude in a setting that was both awesome and elemental. All of which predisposed him toward that which, by ideology and conviction, he did eventually espouse, the ideals of the French Revolution:

> If at the first outbreak I rejoiced
> Less than might well befit my youth, the cause
> In part lay here, that unto me the events
> Seemed nothing out of nature's certain course,
> A gift that rather was come late than soon.

The natural goodness of man he inclined to take for granted, so it did indeed seem possible that the removal of malignant forms of government and the establishment of a benign intercourse between nature and human nature (his own experience suggested that this *was* benign) could lead to a regeneration of the world. Certainly when Wordsworth and his friend Robert Jones went on a walking tour through France in 1790, the summer after the fall of the Bastille, they could not miss the atmosphere of festival and the feeling that the country had awakened.

> *Jones! as from Calais southward you and I*
> *Went pacing side by side, this public Way*
> *Streamed with the pomp of a too-credulous day,*
> *When faith was pledged to new-born Liberty:*
> *A homeless sound of joy was in the sky:*
> *From hour to hour the antiquated Earth*
> *Beat like the heart of Man: songs, garlands, mirth,*
> *Banners, and happy faces, far and nigh!*

These possibilities were even more assiduously debated and espoused when he returned to France a year later and spent a further twelve months in the neighborhood of Blois and Orléans. Two things of crucial import happened then. He had an affair with Annette Vallon, the daughter of Royalist parents in mainly Royalist Blois, and had a child by her; and he met the charismatic revolutionary officer, Michel Beaupuy, who converted him emotionally to the cause of the new regime. Everything seemed to be opening up along the grain of good expectation. His sexuality, his politics, his predisposition to trust in the reliability of people and in the general summeriness of reality, all looked like being fulfilled.

Wordsworth certainly had hopes of marrying Annette, although when he returned to England, war was declared upon revolutionary France and his access to her was suddenly blocked. Ten years later, at a highly charged moment which produced the magnificent sonnets of 1802, he

would cross to Calais to meet his daughter Caroline and her mother, a journey taken openly and conscientiously, to make emotional and no doubt legal settlements before he would wed Mary Hutchinson. But for the moment, the country of the enemy and the home of the beloved had become synonymous. Moreover, his political sympathies still lay with the Revolution: back in that English land he had so cherished, both as the physical nurse of his being and the traditional guardian of liberty, he felt like a traitor. And then, as if this self-division were not enough, his commitment to the justice of the French cause was cast into doubt by the newly violent course of events in Paris, culminating in the Reign of Terror. All this, which he describes in books X and XI of *The Prelude,* drove him into the realms of philosophic and political theory, in particular to the unremittingly rational works of William Godwin, a philosopher whose indifference to the submerged emotional needs of the human being was bound to be at odds with the deepest recognitions of Wordsworth's own nature. At an extreme of bewilderment and exhaustion he then "yielded up moral questions in despair."

Wordsworth had at this point written two typically Augustan poems, full of the poetic diction he would eventually scorn, and set in landscapes (the Alps and the Lake District) he would soon celebrate in a very different kind of poem. The writing of these works was, in the prim sense of the word, an accomplishment, a display of skills in the polite art of verse. The poetry he now embarked upon, under the influence of Dorothy and of Coleridge, was far more fundamentally questioning and urgent. It did not concede anything to ornament, but entered upon imaginative composition as a way of knowledge. This new poetry sought to look destitution, of body and spirit, in the eye; to regard it with sympathy, not be be dumbfounded or discouraged by it, yet not to be calloused against it; and narratives such as "The Ruined Cottage," "Goody Blake and Harry Gill," and "Michael" are the great first heft of this effort. It also sought consciously to retrieve for the chastened adult consciousness the spontaneous, trustful energies unconsciously available in the world of childhood. Memory in this poetry became not

just an inert coffer of images, but a great projector of enabling light. When such a faculty, therefore, was exercised by a mind formed through experiences of the beautiful and fearful aspects of nature, it became life-saving. And such is the great theme of "Tintern Abbey," *The Prelude,* and "The Excursion."

Having crested upon the powers he had summoned by the act of writing, it was Wordsworth's destiny to contemplate the ebb of those powers and the flight of that vision. Yet he had schooled himself in the discipline of maintaining equanimity in the face of loss, and the ultimate rewards of this habit of patience are to be found in masterpieces of disappointment like the "Immortality Ode" and "Elegiac Stanzas." But equally the reader rejoices in the occasional full-throated cry of hurt, so immediate—as in "Extempore Effusion"—that one wishes it would overflow the imposition of his customary resignation.

"Chearfulness," a robust, committed, and justifiably positive attitude in the face of evil and injustice, a comprehension that could acknowledge the ubiquity and affront of pain while yet permitting itself to be visited without anxiety by pleasure—this was the goal of Wordsworth's quest in the 1790s and its meaning for our lives in the 1980s is no less central. Equally instructive, however, is the gradual atrophy we perceive in him as the Romantic quester mutates into the Victorian eminence, and an achieved calm turns into an impregnable placidity. The implacably equable conservative, full of self-warming trust that everybody else can adjust to and succeed in a world where he—and he will be glad to tell you how—has succeeded; this figure with whom we grow all too familiar is also presaged in Wordsworth, but only in the inessential Wordsworth. The essential poet remains the one struggling to become a whole person, to reconcile a sense of incoherence and disappointment forced upon him by the external circumstances of life with those intimations of harmonious communion promised by his childhood visions, and seemingly ratified by his glimpse of a society trembling at the moment of revolution.

Because of the limited space available, certain longish works I would have liked to include have had to be excluded; for example, "The Idiot Boy" or "The Thorn" would have reinforced the "ballad" aspect of *Lyrical Ballads;* and the account of the Pedlar in Book First of "The Excursion" would have revealed how Wordsworth, once he had discerned a pattern to his development, began to project and idealize his own experience.

Except for "The Ruined Cottage" and the sections devoted to *The Prelude,* the poems here are reprinted from John O. Hayden's two-volume edition of *The Poems* (Penguin Books, 1977; Yale University Press, 1981). The order is also that established by Hayden, again with those exceptions already noted. I thought it proper to separate "The Two-Part Prelude" from other poems written at the same time, and have therefore placed extracts from the 1802 Preface as a sort of coda to the shorter poems of the late 1790s. *Lyrical Ballads,* after all, had been the result of a distinct creative project, previous to the autobiographical enterprise of late 1799. It also seemed appropriate to follow the 1799 version with the other excerpts from the 1805 *Prelude.* These are taken from Ernest de Selincourt's edition, revised by Helen Darbishire (Oxford University Press, 1960); "The Two-Part Prelude" and "The Ruined Cottage" are reprinted from Jonathan Wordsworth's two invaluable critical editions of these and other poems, published by Cambridge University Press in 1985. I have been deeply indebted to these editors, first as a reader and now as the compiler of this selection.

—SEAMUS HEANEY

POEMS

Written in Very Early Youth

Calm is all nature as a resting wheel.
The kine are couched upon the dewy grass;
The horse alone, seen dimly as I pass,
Is cropping audibly his later meal:
Dark is the ground; a slumber seems to steal
O'er vale, and mountain, and the starless sky.
Now, in this blank of things, a harmony,
Home-felt, and home-created, comes to heal
That grief for which the senses still supply
Fresh food; for only then, when memory
Is hushed, am I at rest. My Friends! restrain
Those busy cares that would allay my pain;
Oh! leave me to myself, nor let me feel
The officious touch that makes me droop again.

The Ruined Cottage

FIRST PART

'Twas Summer and the sun was mounted high;
Along the south the uplands feebly glared
Through a pale steam, and all the northern downs,
In clearer air ascending, shewed far off
Their surfaces with shadows dappled o'er

Of deep embattled clouds. Far as the sight
Could reach those many shadows lay in spots
Determined and unmoved, with steady beams
Of clear and pleasant sunshine interposed—
Pleasant to him who on the soft cool moss
Extends his careless limbs beside the root
Of some huge oak whose aged branches make
A twilight of their own, a dewy shade
Where the wren warbles while the dreaming man,
Half-conscious of that soothing melody,
With side-long eye looks out upon the scene,
By those impending branches made more soft,
More soft and distant.
                              Other lot was mine.
Across a bare wide common I had toiled
With languid feet which by the slippery ground
Were baffled still; and when I stretched myself
On the brown earth my limbs from very heat
Could find no rest, nor my weak arm disperse
The insect host which gathered round my face
And joined their murmurs to the tedious noise
Of seeds of bursting gorse that crackled round.
I rose and turned towards a group of trees
Which midway in that level stood alone;
And thither come at length, beneath a shade
Of clustering elms that sprang from the same root
I found a ruined house, four naked walls
That stared upon each other. I looked round,
And near the door I saw an aged man
Alone and stretched upon the cottage bench;
An iron-pointed staff lay at his side.
With instantanious joy I recognized
That pride of Nature and of lowly life,
The venerable Armytage, a friend

As dear to me as is the setting sun.
                        Two days before
We had been fellow-travellers. I knew
That he was in this neighbourhood, and now
Delighted found him here in the cool shade.
He lay, his pack of rustic merchandize
Pillowing his head. I guess he had no thought
Of his way-wandering life. His eyes were shut,
The shadows of the breezy elms above
Dappled his face. With thirsty heat oppressed
At length I hailed him, glad to see his hat
Bedewed with water-drops, as if the brim
Had newly scooped a running stream. He rose
And pointing to a sun-flower, bade me climb
The [   ] wall where that same gaudy flower
Looked out upon the road.
                        It was a plot
Of garden-ground now wild, its matted weeds
Marked with the steps of those whom as they passed,
The gooseberry-trees that shot in long lank slips,
Or currants hanging from their leafless stems
In scanty strings, had tempted to o'erleap
The broken wall. Within that cheerless spot,
Where two tall hedgerows of thick alder boughs
Joined in a damp cold nook, I found a well
Half covered up with willow-flowers and grass.
I slaked my thirst and to the shady bench
Returned, and while I stood unbonneted
To catch the motion of the cooler air
The old man said, 'I see around me here
Things which you cannot see. We die, my friend,
Nor we alone, but that which each man loved
And prized in his peculiar nook of earth
Dies with him, or is changed, and very soon

Even of the good is no memorial left.
The poets, in their elegies and songs
Lamenting the departed, call the groves,
They call upon the hills and streams to mourn,
And senseless rocks—nor idly, for they speak
In these their invocations with a voice
Obedient to the strong creative power
Of human passion. Sympathies there are
More tranquil, yet perhaps of kindred birth,
That steal upon the meditative mind
And grow with thought. Beside yon spring I stood,
And eyed its waters till we seemed to feel
One sadness, they and I. For them a bond
Of brotherhood is broken: time has been
When every day the touch of human hand
Disturbed their stillness, and they ministered
To human comfort. When I stooped to drink
A spider's web hung to the water's edge,
And on the wet and slimy foot-stone lay
The useless fragment of a wooden bowl.
It moved my very heart.

              The day has been
When I could never pass this road but she
Who lived within these walls, when I appeared,
A daughter's welcome gave me, and I loved her
As my own child. Oh sir, the good die first,
And they whose hearts are dry as summer dust
Burn to the socket. Many a passenger
Has blessed poor Margaret for her gentle looks
When she upheld the cool refreshment drawn
From that forsaken spring, and no one came
But he was welcome, no one went away
But that it seemed she loved him. She is dead,
The worm is on her cheek, and this poor hut,

Stripped of its outward garb of household flowers,
Of rose and sweetbriar, offers to the wind
A cold bare wall whose earthy top is tricked
With weeds and the rank speargrass. She is dead,
And nettles rot and adders sun themselves
Where we have sate together while she nursed
Her infant at her breast. The unshod colt,
The wandering heifer and the potter's ass,
Find shelter now within the chimney-wall
Where I have seen her evening hearthstone blaze
And through the window spread upon the road
Its chearful light. You will forgive me, sir,
But often on this cottage do I muse
As on a picture, till my wiser mind
Sinks, yielding to the foolishness of grief.

   She had a husband, an industrious man,
Sober and steady. I have heard her say
That he was up and busy at his loom
In summer ere the mower's scythe had swept
The dewy grass, and in the early spring
Ere the last star had vanished. They who passed
At evening, from behind the garden-fence
Might hear his busy spade, which he would ply
After his daily work till the daylight
Was gone, and every leaf and flower were lost
In the dark hedges. So they passed their days
In peace and comfort, and two pretty babes
Were their best hope next to the God in heaven.

   You may remember, now some ten years gone,
Two blighting seasons when the fields were left
With half a harvest. It pleased heaven to add
A worse affliction in the plague of war;
A happy land was stricken to the heart—
'Twas a sad time of sorrow and distress.

A wanderer among the cottages,
I with my pack of winter raiment saw
The hardships of that season. Many rich
Sunk down as in a dream among the poor,
And of the poor did many cease to be,
And their place knew them not. Meanwhile, abridged
Of daily comforts, gladly reconciled
To numerous self-denials, Margaret
Went struggling on through those calamitous years
With chearful hope. But ere the second autumn,
A fever seized her husband. In disease
He lingered long, and when his strength returned
He found the little he had stored to meet
The hour of accident, or crippling age,
Was all consumed. As I have said, 'twas now
A time of trouble: shoals of artisans
Were from their daily labour turned away
To hang for bread on parish charity,
They and their wives and children—happier far
Could they have lived as do the little birds
That peck along the hedges, or the kite
That makes her dwelling in the mountain rocks.

  Ill fared it now with Robert, he who dwelt
In this poor cottage. At his door he stood
And whistled many a snatch of merry tunes
That had no mirth in them, or with his knife
Carved uncouth figures on the heads of sticks;
Then idly sought about through every nook
Of house or garden any casual task
Of use or ornament, and with a strange
Amusing but uneasy novelty
He blended where he might the various tasks
Of summer, autumn, winter, and of spring.
But this endured not, his good humour soon

Became a weight in which no pleasure was,
And poverty brought on a petted mood
And a sore temper. Day by day he drooped,
And he would leave his home, and to the town
Without an errand would he turn his steps,
Or wander here and there among the fields.
One while he would speak lightly of his babes
And with a cruel tongue; at other times
He played with them wild freaks of merriment,
And 'twas a piteous thing to see the looks
Of the poor innocent children. "Every smile",
Said Margaret to me here beneath these trees,
"Made my heart bleed."

                              At this the old man paused,
And looking up to those enormous elms
He said, " 'Tis now the hour of deepest noon.
At this still season of repose and peace,
This hour when all things which are not at rest
Are chearful, while this multitude of flies
Fills all the air with happy melody,
Why should a tear be in an old man's eye?
Why should we thus with an untoward mind,
And in the weakness of humanity,
From natural wisdom turn our hearts away,
To natural comfort shut our eyes and ears,
And feeding on disquiet, thus disturb
The calm of Nature with our restless thoughts?"

SECOND PART

He spake with somewhat of a solemn tone,
But when he ended there was in his face
Such easy chearfulness, a look so mild,
That for a little time it stole away

All recollection, and that simple tale
Passed from my mind like a forgotten sound.
A while on trivial things we held discourse,
To me soon tasteless. In my own despite
I thought of that poor woman as of one
Whom I had known and loved. He had rehearsed
Her homely tale with such familiar power,
With such an active countenance, an eye
So busy, that the things of which he spake
Seemed present, and, attention now relaxed,
There was a heartfelt chillness in my veins.
I rose, and turning from that breezy shade
Went out into the open air, and stood
To drink the comfort of the warmer sun.
Long time I had not stayed ere, looking round
Upon that tranquil ruin, I returned
And begged of the old man that for my sake
He would resume his story.
                              He replied,
"It were a wantonness, and would demand
Severe reproof, if we were men whose hearts
Could hold vain dalliance with the misery
Even of the dead, contented thence to draw
A momentary pleasure, never marked
By reason, barren of all future good.
But we have known that there is often found
In mournful thoughts, and always might be found,
A power to virtue friendly; were't not so
I am a dreamer among men, indeed
An idle dreamer. 'Tis a common tale
By moving accidents uncharactered,
A tale of silent suffering, hardly clothed
In bodily form, and to the grosser sense
But ill adapted—scarcely palpable

To him who does not think. But at your bidding
I will proceed.

        While thus it fared with them
To whom this cottage till that hapless year
Had been a blessed home, it was my chance
To travel in a country far remote;
And glad I was when, halting by yon gate
That leads from the green lane, again I saw
These lofty elm-trees. Long I did not rest—
With many pleasant thoughts I cheered my way
O'er the flat common. At the door arrived,
I knocked, and when I entered, with the hope
Of usual greeting, Margaret looked at me
A little while, then turned her head away
Speechless, and sitting down upon a chair
Wept bitterly. I wist not what to do,
Or how to speak to her. Poor wretch, at last
She rose from off her seat, and then, oh sir,
I cannot tell how she pronounced my name.
With fervent love, and with a face of grief
Unutterably helpless, and a look
That seemed to cling upon me, she enquired
If I had seen her husband. As she spake
A strange surprise and fear came to my heart,
Nor had I power to answer ere she told
That he had disappeared—just two months gone
He left his house: two wretched days had passed,
And on the third by the first break of light,
Within her casement full in view she saw
A purse of gold. "I trembled at the sight,"
Said Margaret, "for I knew it was his hand
That placed it there. And on that very day
By one, a stranger, from my husband sent,
The tidings came that he had joined a troop

Of soldiers going to a distant land.
He left me thus. Poor man, he had not heart
To take a farewell of me, and he feared
That I should follow with my babes, and sink
Beneath the misery of a soldier's life."

      This tale did Margaret tell with many tears,
And when she ended I had little power
To give her comfort, and was glad to take
Such words of hope from her own mouth as served
To cheer us both. But long we had not talked
Ere we built up a pile of better thoughts,
And with a brighter eye she looked around
As if she had been shedding tears of joy.
We parted. It was then the early spring;
I left her busy with her garden tools,
And well remember, o'er that fence she looked,
And, while I paced along the foot-way path,
Called out and sent a blessing after me,
With tender chearfulness, and with a voice
That seemed the very sound of happy thoughts.

      I roved o'er many a hill and many a dale
With this my weary load, in heat and cold,
Through many a wood and many an open ground,
In sunshine or in shade, in wet or fair,
Now blithe, now drooping, as it might befal;
My best companions now the driving winds
And now the "trotting brooks" and whispering trees,
And now the music of my own sad steps,
With many a short-lived thought that passed between
And disappeared.

            I came this way again
Towards the wane of summer, when the wheat
Was yellow, and the soft and bladed grass
Sprang up afresh and o'er the hayfield spread

Its tender green. When I had reached the door
I found that she was absent. In the shade,
Where we now sit, I waited her return.
Her cottage in its outward look appeared
As chearful as before, in any shew
Of neatness little changed—but that I thought
The honeysuckle crowded round the door
And from the wall hung down in heavier tufts,
And knots of worthless stonecrop started out
Along the window's edge, and grew like weeds
Against the lower panes. I turned aside
And strolled into her garden. It was changed.
The unprofitable bindweed spread his bells
From side to side, and with unwieldy wreaths
Had dragged the rose from its sustaining wall
And bent it down to earth. The border tufts,
Daisy, and thrift, and lowly camomile,
And thyme, had straggled out into the paths
Which they were used to deck.

                                        Ere this an hour
Was wasted. Back I turned my restless steps,
And as I walked before the door it chanced
A stranger passed, and guessing whom I sought,
He said that she was used to ramble far.
The sun was sinking in the west, and now
I sate with sad impatience. From within
Her solitary infant cried aloud.
The spot though fair seemed very desolate—
The longer I remained more desolate—
And looking round I saw the corner-stones,
Till then unmarked, on either side the door
With dull red stains discoloured, and stuck o'er
With tufts and hairs of wool, as if the sheep
That feed upon the commons thither came

Familiarly, and found a couching-place
Even at her threshold.
                        The house-clock struck eight:
I turned and saw her distant a few steps.
Her face was pale and thin, her figure too
Was changed. As she unlocked the door she said,
"It grieves me you have waited here so long,
But in good truth I've wandered much of late,
And sometimes—to my shame I speak—have need
Of my best prayers to bring me back again."
While on the board she spread our evening meal
She told me she had lost her elder child,
That he for months had been a serving-boy,
Apprenticed by the parish. "I perceive
You look at me, and you have cause. Today
I have been travelling far, and many days
About the fields I wander, knowing this
Only, that what I seek I cannot find.
And so I waste my time: for I am changed,
And to myself", said she, "have done much wrong,
And to this helpless infant. I have slept
Weeping, and weeping I have waked. My tears
Have flowed as if my body were not such
As others are, and I could never die.
But I am now in mind and in my heart
More easy, and I hope", said she, "that heaven
Will give me patience to endure the things
Which I behold at home."
                        It would have grieved
Your very soul to see her. Sir, I feel
The story linger in my heart. I fear
'Tis long and tedious, but my spirit clings
To that poor woman. So familiarly
Do I perceive her manner and her look

And presence, and so deeply do I feel
Her goodness, that not seldom in my walks
A momentary trance comes over me
And to myself I seem to muse on one
By sorrow laid asleep or borne away,
A human being destined to awake
To human life, or something very near
To human life, when he shall come again
For whom she suffered. Sir, it would have grieved
Your very soul to see her: evermore
Her eyelids drooped, her eyes were downward cast,
And when she at her table gave me food
She did not look at me. Her voice was low,
Her body was subdued. In every act
Pertaining to her house-affairs appeared
The careless stillness which a thinking mind
Gives to an idle matter. Still she sighed,
But yet no motion of the breast was seen,
No heaving of the heart. While by the fire
We sate together, sighs came on my ear—
I knew not how, and hardly whence, they came.
I took my staff, and when I kissed her babe
The tears stood in her eyes. I left her then
With the best hope and comfort I could give:
She thanked me for my will, but for my hope
It seemed she did not thank me.
                                        I returned
And took my rounds along this road again
Ere on its sunny bank the primrose flower
Had chronicled the earliest day of spring.
I found her sad and drooping. She had learned
No tidings of her husband. If he lived,
She knew not that he lived: if he were dead,
She knew not he was dead. She seemed the same

In person or appearance, but her house
Bespoke a sleepy hand of negligence.
The floor was neither dry nor neat, the hearth
Was comfortless,
The windows too were dim, and her few books,
Which one upon the other heretofore
Had been piled up against the corner-panes
In seemly order, now with straggling leaves
Lay scattered here and there, open or shut,
As they had chanced to fall. Her infant babe
Had from its mother caught the trick of grief,
And sighed among its playthings. Once again
I turned towards the garden-gate, and saw
More plainly still that poverty and grief
Were now come nearer to her. The earth was hard
With weeds defaced and knots of withered grass;
No ridges there appeared of clear black mould,
No winter greenness. Of her herbs and flowers
It seemed the better part were gnawed away
Or trampled on the earth. A chain of straw,
Which had been twisted round the tender stem
Of a young appletree, lay at its root;
The bark was nibbled round by truant sheep.
Margaret stood near, her infant in her arms,
And, seeing that my eye was on the tree,
She said, "I fear it will be dead and gone
Ere Robert come again."
                       Towards the house
Together we returned, and she inquired
If I had any hope. But for her babe,
And for her little friendless boy, she said,
She had no wish to live—that she must die
Of sorrow. Yet I saw the idle loom
Still in its place. His Sunday garments hung

Upon the self-same nail, his very staff
Stood undisturbed behind the door. And when
I passed this way beaten by autumn winds,
She told me that her little babe was dead
And she was left alone. That very time,
I yet remember, through the miry lane
She walked with me a mile, when the bare trees
Trickled with foggy damps, and in such sort
That any heart had ached to hear her, begged
That wheresoe'er I went I still would ask
For him whom she had lost. We parted then,
Our final parting; for from that time forth
Did many seasons pass ere I returned
Into this tract again.
                Five tedious years
She lingered in unquiet widowhood,
A wife and widow. Needs must it have been
A sore heart-wasting. I have heard, my friend,
That in that broken arbour she would sit
The idle length of half a sabbath day—
There, where you see the toadstool's lazy head—
And when a dog passed by she still would quit
The shade and look abroad. On this old bench
For hours she sate, and evermore her eye
Was busy in the distance, shaping things
Which made her heart beat quick. Seest thou that path?—
The green-sward now has broken its grey line—
There to and fro she paced through many a day
Of the warm summer, from a belt of flax
That girt her waist, spinning the long-drawn thread
With backward steps. Yet ever as there passed
A man whose garments shewed the soldier's red,
Or crippled mendicant in sailor's garb,
The little child who sate to turn the wheel

Ceased from his toil, and she, with faltering voice,
Expecting still to learn her husband's fate,
Made many a fond inquiry; and when they
Whose presence gave no comfort were gone by,
Her heart was still more sad. And by yon gate,
Which bars the traveller's road, she often stood,
And when a stranger horseman came, the latch
Would lift, and in his face look wistfully,
Most happy if from aught discovered there
Of tender feeling she might dare repeat
The same sad question.
                              Meanwhile her poor hut
Sunk to decay; for he was gone, whose hand
At the first nippings of October frost
Closed up each chink, and with fresh bands of straw
Chequered the green-grown thatch. And so she lived
Through the long winter, reckless and alone,
Till this reft house, by frost, and thaw, and rain,
Was sapped; and when she slept, the nightly damps
Did chill her breast, and in the stormy day
Her tattered clothes were ruffled by the wind
Even at the side of her own fire. Yet still
She loved this wretched spot, nor would for worlds
Have parted hence; and still that length of road,
And this rude bench, one torturing hope endeared,
Fast rooted at her heart. And here, my friend,
In sickness she remained; and here she died,
Last human tenant of these ruined walls.'

        The old man ceased; he saw that I was moved.
From that low Bench rising instinctively
I turned aside in weakness, nor had power
To thank him for the tale which he had told.
I stood, and leaning o'er the garden gate
Reviewed that woman's sufferings; and it seemed

To comfort me while with a brother's love
I blessed her in the impotence of grief.
At length towards the cottage I returned
Fondly, and traced with milder interest
That secret spirit of humanity
Which, mid the calm oblivious tendencies
Of Nature, mid her plants, her weeds and flowers,
And silent overgrowings, still survived.
The old man seeing this resumed, and said,
'My friend, enough to sorrow have you given,
The purposes of wisdom ask no more:
Be wise and chearful, and no longer read
The forms of things with an unworthy eye:
She sleeps in the calm earth, and peace is here.
I well remember that those very plumes,
Those weeds, and the high speargrass on that wall,
By mist and silent raindrops silvered o'er,
As once I passed did to my mind convey
So still an image of tranquility,
So calm and still, and looked so beautiful
Amid the uneasy thoughts which filled my mind,
That what we feel of sorrow and despair
From ruin and from change, and all the grief
The passing shews of being leave behind,
Appeared an idle dream that could not live
Where meditation was. I turned away,
And walked along my road in happiness.'

    He ceased. By this the sun declining shot
A slant and mellow radiance, which began
To fall upon us where beneath the trees
We sate on that low bench. And now we felt,
Admonished thus, the sweet hour coming on:
A linnet warbled from those lofty elms,
A thrush sang loud, and other melodies

At distance heard peopled the milder air.
The old man rose and hoisted up his load;
Together casting then a farewell look
Upon those silent walls, we left the shade,
And ere the stars were visible attained
A rustic inn, our evening resting-place.

Animal Tranquillity and Decay

The little hedgerow birds,
That peck along the road, regard him not.
He travels on, and in his face, his step,
His gait, is one expression: every limb,
His look and bending figure, all bespeak
A man who does not move with pain, but moves
With thought.——He is insensibly subdued
To settled quiet: he is one by whom
All effort seems forgotten; one to whom
Long patience hath such mild composure given,
That patience now doth seem a thing of which
He hath no need. He is by nature led
To peace so perfect that the young behold
With envy, what the Old Man hardly feels.

Fragment: Yet once again

Yet once again do I behold the forms
Of these huge mountains, and yet once again,
Standing beneath these elms, I hear thy voice,
Beloved Derwent, that peculiar voice
Heard in the stillness of the evening air,
Half-heard and half-created.

Fragments from the Alfoxden Notebook (I)

I

there would he stand
In the still covert of some [lonesome?] rock,
Or gaze upon the moon until its light
Fell like a strain of music on his soul
And seemed to sink into his very heart.

II

Why is it we feel
So little for each other, but for this,
That we with nature have no sympathy,
Or with such things as have no power to hold
Articulate language?

And never for each other shall we feel
As we may feel, till we have sympathy
With nature in her forms inanimate,
With objects such as have no power to hold
Articulate language. In all forms of things
There is a mind

III

Of unknown modes of being which on earth,
Or in the heavens, or in the heavens and earth
Exist by mighty combinations, bound
Together by a link, and with a soul
Which makes all one.

To gaze
On that green hill and on those scattered trees

And feel a pleasant consciousness of life
In the impression of that loveliness
Until the sweet sensation called the mind
Into itself, by image from without
Unvisited, and all her reflex powers
Wrapped in a still dream [?of] forgetfulness.

I lived without the knowledge that I lived
Then by those beauteous forms brought back again
To lose myself again as if my life
Did ebb and flow with a strange mystery.

To My Sister

It is the first mild day of March:
Each minute sweeter than before,
The redbreast sings from the tall larch
That stands beside our door.

There is a blessing in the air,
Which seems a sense of joy to yield
To the bare trees, and mountains bare,
And grass in the green field.

My sister! ('tis a wish of mine)
Now that our morning meal is done,
Make haste, your morning task resign;
Come forth and feel the sun.

Edward will come with you;—and, pray,
Put on with speed your woodland dress;
And bring no book: for this one day
We'll give to idleness.

No joyless forms shall regulate
Out living calendar:
We from today, my Friend, will date
The opening of the year.

Love, now a universal birth,
From heart to heart is stealing,
From earth to man, from man to earth:
—It is the hour of feeling.

One moment now may give us more
Than years of toiling reason:
Our minds shall drink at every pore
The spirit of the season.

Some silent laws our hearts will make,
Which they shall long obey:
We for the year to come may take
Our temper from today.

And from the blessed power that rolls
About, below, above,
We'll frame the measure of our souls:
They shall be tuned to love.

Then come, my Sister! come, I pray,
With speed put on your woodland dress;
And bring no book: for this one day
We'll give to idleness.

Goody Blake and Harry Gill

A TRUE STORY

Oh! what's the matter? what's the matter?
What is't that ails young Harry Gill?
That evermore his teeth they chatter,
Chatter, chatter, chatter still!
Of waistcoats Harry has no lack,
Good duffle grey, and flannel fine;
He has a blanket on his back,
And coats enough to smother nine.

In March, December, and in July,
'Tis all the same with Harry Gill;
The neighbours tell, and tell you truly,
His teeth they chatter, chatter still.
At night, at morning, and at noon,
'Tis all the same with Harry Gill;
Beneath the sun, beneath the moon,
His teeth they chatter, chatter still!

Young Harry was a lusty drover,
And who so stout of limb as he?
His cheeks were red as ruddy clover;
His voice was like the voice of three.
Old Goody Blake was old and poor;
Ill fed she was, and thinly clad;
And any man who passed her door
Might see how poor a hut she had.

All day she spun in her poor dwelling:
And then her three hours' work at night,
Alas! 'twas hardly worth the telling,

It would not pay for candle-light.
Remote from sheltered village-green,
On a hill's northern side she dwelt,
Where from sea-blasts the hawthorns lean,
And hoary dews are slow to melt.

By the same fire to boil their pottage,
Two poor old Dames, as I have known,
Will often live in one small cottage;
But she, poor Woman! housed alone.
'Twas well enough, when summer came,
The long, warm, lightsome summer-day,
Then at her door the *canty* Dame
Would sit, as any linnet, gay.

But when the ice our streams did fetter,
Oh then how her old bones would shake!
You would have said, if you had met her,
'Twas a hard time for Goody Blake.
Her evenings then were dull and dead:
Sad case it was, as you may think,
For very cold to go to bed;
And then for cold not sleep a wink.

O joy for her! whene'er in winter
The winds at night had made a rout;
And scattered many a lusty splinter
And many a rotten bough about.
Yet never had she, well or sick,
As every man who knew her says,
A pile beforehand, turf or stick,
Enough to warm her for three days.

Now, when the frost was past enduring,
And made her poor old bones to ache,
Could any thing be more alluring
Than an old hedge to Goody Blake?
And, now and then, it must be said,
When her old bones were cold and chill,
She left her fire, or left her bed,
To seek the hedge of Harry Gill.

Now Harry he had long suspected
This trespass of old Goody Blake;
And vowed that she should be detected—
That he on her would vengeance take.
And oft from his warm fire he'd go,
And to the fields his road would take;
And there, at night, in frost and snow,
He watched to seize old Goody Blake.

And once, behind a rick of barley,
Thus looking out did Harry stand:
The moon was full and shining clearly,
And crisp with frost the stubble land.
—He hears a noise—he's all awake—
Again?—on tip-toe down the hill
He softly creeps—'tis Goody Blake;
She's at the hedge of Harry Gill!

Right glad was he when he beheld her:
Stick after stick did Goody pull:
He stood behind a bush of elder,
Till she had filled her apron full.
When with her load she turned about,
The by-way back again to take;

He started forward, with a shout,
And sprang upon poor Goody Blake.

And fiercely by the arm he took her,
And by the arm he held her fast,
And fiercely by the arm he shook her,
And cried, 'I've caught you then at last!'
Then Goody, who had nothing said,
Her bundle from her lap let fall;
And, kneeling on the sticks, she prayed
To God that is the judge of all.

She prayed, her withered hand uprearing,
While Harry held her by the arm—
'God! who art never out of hearing,
O may he never more be warm!'
The cold, cold moon above her head,
Thus on her knees did Goody pray;
Young Harry heard what she had said:
And icy cold he turned away.

He went complaining all the morrow
That he was cold and very chill:
His face was gloom, his heart was sorrow,
Alas! that day for Harry Gill!
That day he wore a riding-coat,
But not a whit the warmer he:
Another was on Thursday brought,
And ere the Sabbath he had three.

'Twas all in vain, a useless matter,
And blankets were about him pinned;
Yet still his jaws and teeth they clatter,
Like a loose casement in the wind.

And Harry's flesh it fell away;
And all who see him say, 'tis plain,
That, live as long as live he may,
He never will be warm again.

No word to any man he utters,
A-bed or up, to young or old;
But ever to himself he mutters,
'Poor Harry Gill is very cold.'
A-bed or up, by night or day;
His teeth they chatter, chatter still.
Now think, ye farmers all, I pray,
Of Goody Blake and Harry Gill!

Lines Written in Early Spring

I heard a thousand blended notes,
While in a grove I sate reclined,
In that sweet mood when pleasant thoughts
Bring sad thoughts to the mind.

To her fair works did Nature link
The human soul that through me ran;
And much it grieved my heart to think
What man has made of man.

Through primrose tufts, in that green bower,
The periwinkle trailed its wreaths;
And 'tis my faith that every flower
Enjoys the air it breathes.

The birds around me hopped and played,
Their thoughts I cannot measure:—

But the least motion which they made,
It seemed a thrill of pleasure.

The budding twigs spread out their fan,
To catch the breezy air;
And I must think, do all I can,
That there was pleasure there.

If this belief from heaven be sent,
If such be Nature's holy plan,
Have I not reason to lament
What man has made of man?

Expostulation and Reply

'Why, William, on that old grey stone,
Thus for the length of half a day,
Why, William, sit you thus alone,
And dream your time away?

'Where are your books?—that light bequeathed
To Beings else forlorn and blind!
Up! up! and drink the spirit breathed
From dead men to their kind.

'You look round on your Mother Earth,
As if she for no purpose bore you;
As if you were her first-born birth,
And none had lived before you!'

One morning thus, by Esthwaite lake,
When life was sweet, I knew not why,

To me my good friend Matthew spake,
And thus I made reply:

'The eye—it cannot choose but see;
We cannot bid the ear be still;
Our bodies feel, where'er they be,
Against or with our will.

'Nor less I deem that there are Powers
Which of themselves our minds impress;
That we can feed this mind of ours
In a wise passiveness.

'Think you, 'mid all this mighty sum
Of things for ever speaking,
That nothing of itself will come,
But we must still be seeking?

'—Then ask not wherefore, here, alone,
Conversing as I may,
I sit upon this old grey stone,
And dream my time away.'

The Tables Turned

AN EVENING SCENE ON THE SAME SUBJECT

Up! up! my Friend, and quit your books;
Or surely you'll grow double:
Up! up! my Friend, and clear your looks;
Why all this toil and trouble?

The sun, above the mountain's head,
A freshening lustre mellow
Through all the long green fields has spread,
His first sweet evening yellow.

Books! 'tis a dull and endless strife:
Come, hear the woodland linnet,
How sweet his music! on my life,
There's more of wisdom in it.

And hark! how blithe the throstle sings!
He, too, is no mean preacher:
Come forth into the light of things,
Let Nature be your Teacher.

She has a world of ready wealth,
Our minds and hearts to bless—
Spontaneous wisdom breathed by health,
Truth breathed by cheerfulness.

One impulse from a vernal wood
May teach you more of man,
Of moral evil and of good,
Than all the sages can.

Sweet is the lore which Nature brings;
Our meddling intellect
Mis-shapes the beauteous forms of things:—
We murder to dissect.

Enough of Science and of Art;
Close up those barren leaves;
Come forth, and bring with you a heart
That watches and receives.

*Lines Composed a Few Miles above Tintern Abbey,
on Revisiting the Banks of the Wye
during a Tour. July 13, 1798*

Five years have past; five summers, with the length
Of five long winters! and again I hear
These waters, rolling from their mountain-springs
With a soft inland murmur.—Once again
Do I behold these steep and lofty cliffs,
That on a wild secluded scene impress
Thoughts of more deep seclusion; and connect
The landscape with the quiet of the sky.
The day is come when I again repose
Here, under this dark sycamore, and view
These plots of cottage-ground, these orchard-tufts,
Which at this season, with their unripe fruits,
Are clad in one green hue, and lose themselves
'Mid groves and copses. Once again I see
These hedge-rows, hardly hedge-rows, little lines
Of sportive wood run wild: these pastoral farms,
Green to the very door; and wreaths of smoke
Sent up, in silence, from among the trees!
With some uncertain notice, as might seem
Of vagrant dwellers in the houseless woods,
Or of some Hermit's cave, where by his fire
The Hermit sits alone.
                            These beauteous forms,
Through a long absence, have not been to me
As is a landscape to a blind man's eye:
But oft, in lonely rooms, and 'mid the din
Of towns and cities, I have owed to them
In hours of weariness, sensations sweet,
Felt in the blood, and felt along the heart;
And passing even into my purer mind,

With tranquil restoration:—feelings too
Of unremembered pleasure: such, perhaps,
As have no slight or trivial influence
On that best portion of a good man's life,
His little, nameless, unremembered, acts
Of kindness and of love. Nor less, I trust,
To them I may have owed another gift,
Of aspect more sublime; that blessed mood,
In which the burden of the mystery,
In which the heavy and the weary weight
Of all this unintelligible world,
Is lightened:—that serene and blessed mood,
In which the affections gently lead us on,—
Until, the breath of this corporeal frame
And even the motion of our human blood
Almost suspended, we are laid asleep
In body, and become a living soul:
While with an eye made quiet by the power
Of harmony, and the deep power of joy,
We see into the life of things.
                                        If this
Be but a vain belief, yet, oh! how oft—
In darkness and amid the many shapes
Of joyless daylight; when the fretful stir
Unprofitable, and the fever of the world,
Have hung upon the beatings of my heart—
How oft, in spirit, have I turned to thee,
O sylvan Wye! thou wanderer through the woods,
How often has my spirit turned to thee!

And now, with gleams of half-extinguished thought,
With many recognitions dim and faint,
And somewhat of a sad perplexity,
The picture of the mind revives again:

While here I stand, not only with the sense
Of present pleasure, but with pleasing thoughts
That in this moment there is life and food
For future years. And so I dare to hope,
Though changed, no doubt, from what I was when first
I came among these hills; when like a roe
I bounded o'er the mountains, by the sides
Of the deep rivers, and the lonely streams,
Wherever nature led: more like a man
Flying from something that he dreads, than one
Who sought the thing he loved. For nature then
(The coarser pleasures of my boyish days,
And their glad animal movements all gone by)
To me was all in all.—I cannot paint
What then I was. The sounding cataract
Haunted me like a passion: the tall rock,
The mountain, and the deep and gloomy wood,
Their colours and their forms, were then to me
An appetite; a feeling and a love,
That had no need of a remoter charm,
By thought supplied, nor any interest
Unborrowed from the eye.—That time is past,
And all its aching joys are now no more,
And all its dizzy raptures. Not for this
Faint I, nor mourn nor murmur; other gifts
Have followed; for such loss, I would believe,
Abundant recompense. For I have learned
To look on nature, not as in the hour
Of thoughtless youth; but hearing oftentimes
The still, sad music of humanity,
Nor harsh nor grating, though of ample power
To chasten and subdue. And I have felt
A presence that disturbs me with the joy
Of elevated thoughts; a sense sublime

Of something far more deeply interfused,
Whose dwelling is the light of setting suns,
And the round ocean and the living air,
And the blue sky, and in the mind of man:
A motion and a spirit, that impels
All thinking things, all objects of all thought,
And rolls through all things. Therefore am I still
A lover of the meadows and the woods,
And mountains; and of all that we behold
From this green earth; of all the mighty world
Of eye, and ear,—both what they half create,
And what perceive; well pleased to recognize
In nature and the language of the sense,
The anchor of my purest thoughts, the nurse,
The guide, the guardian of my heart, and soul
Of all my moral being.
                         Nor perchance,
If I were not thus taught, should I the more
Suffer my genial spirits to decay:
For thou art with me here upon the banks
Of this fair river; thou my dearest Friend,
My dear, dear Friend; and in thy voice I catch
The language of my former heart, and read
My former pleasures in the shooting lights
Of thy wild eyes. Oh! yet a little while
May I behold in thee what I was once,
My dear, dear Sister! and this prayer I make,
Knowing that Nature never did betray
The heart that loved her; 'tis her privilege,
Through all the years of this our life, to lead
From joy to joy: for she can so inform
The mind that is within us, so impress
With quietness and beauty, and so feed
With lofty thoughts, that neither evil tongues,

Rash judgements, nor the sneers of selfish men,
Nor greetings where no kindness is, nor all
The dreary intercourse of daily life,
Shall e'er prevail against us, or disturb
Our cheerful faith, that all which we behold
Is full of blessings. Therefore let the moon
Shine on thee in thy solitary walk;
And let the misty mountain-winds be free
To blow against thee: and, in after years,
When these wild ecstasies shall be matured
Into a sober pleasure; when thy mind
Shall be a mansion for all lovely forms,
Thy memory be as a dwelling-place
For all sweet sounds and harmonies; oh! then,
If solitude, or fear, or pain, or grief,
Should be thy portion, with what healing thoughts
Of tender joy wilt thou remember me,
And these my exhortations! Nor, perchance—
If I should be where I no more can hear
Thy voice, nor catch from thy wild eyes these gleams
Of past existence—wilt thou then forget
That on the banks of this delightful stream
We stood together; and that I, so long
A worshipper of Nature, hither came
Unwearied in that service: rather say
With warmer love—oh! with far deeper zeal
Of holier love. Nor wilt thou then forget,
That after many wanderings, many years
Of absence, these steep woods and lofty cliffs,
And this green pastoral landscape, were to me
More dear, both for themselves and for thy sake!

There Was a Boy

There was a Boy; ye knew him well, ye cliffs
And islands of Winander!—many a time,
At evening, when the earliest stars began
To move along the edges of the hills,
Rising or setting, would he stand alone,
Beneath the trees, or by the glimmering lake;
And there, with fingers interwoven, both hands
Pressed closely palm to palm and to his mouth
Uplifted, he, as through an instrument,
Blew mimic hootings to the silent owls,
That they might answer him.—And they would shout
Across the watery vale, and shout again,
Responsive to his call,—with quivering peals,
And long halloos, and screams, and echoes loud
Redoubled and redoubled; concourse wild
Of jocund din! And, when there came a pause
Of silence such as baffled his best skill:
Then, sometimes, in that silence, while he hung
Listening, a gentle shock of mild surprise
Has carried far into his heart the voice
Of mountain-torrents; or the visible scene
Would enter unawares into his mind
With all its solemn imagery, its rocks,
Its woods, and that uncertain heaven received
Into the bosom of the steady lake.

This boy was taken from his mates, and died
In childhood, ere he was full twelve years old.
Pre-eminent in beauty is the vale
Where he was born and bred: the churchyard hangs
Upon a slope above the village-school;
And, through that churchyard when my way has led
On summer-evenings, I believe, that there

A long half-hour together I have stood
Mute—looking at the grave in which he lies!

A slumber did my spirit seal

A slumber did my spirit seal;
    I had no human fears:
She seemed a thing that could not feel
    The touch of earthly years.

No motion has she now, no force;
    She neither hears nor sees;
Rolled round in earth's diurnal course,
    With rocks, and stones, and trees.

She dwelt among the untrodden ways

She dwelt among the untrodden ways
    Beside the springs of Dove,
A Maid whom there were none to praise
    And very few to love:

A violet by a mossy stone
    Half hidden from the eye!
—Fair as a star, when only one
    Is shining in the sky.

She lived unknown, and few could know
    When Lucy ceased to be;
But she is in her grave, and, oh,
    The difference to me!

Strange fits of passion have I known

Strange fits of passion have I known:
And I will dare to tell,
But in the Lover's ear alone,
What once to me befell.

When she I loved looked every day
Fresh as a rose in June,
I to her cottage bent my way,
Beneath an evening moon.

Upon the moon I fixed my eye,
All over the wide lea;
With quickening pace my horse drew nigh
Those paths so dear to me.

And now we reached the orchard-plot;
And, as we climbed the hill,
The sinking moon to Lucy's cot
Came near, and nearer still.

In one of those sweet dreams I slept,
Kind Nature's gentlest boon!
And all the while my eyes I kept
On the descending moon.

My horse moved on; hoof after hoof
He raised, and never stopped:
When down behind the cottage roof,
At once, the bright moon dropped.

What fond and wayward thoughts will slide
Into a Lover's head!

'O mercy!' to myself I cried,
'If Lucy should be dead!'

Nutting

It seems a day
(I speak of one from many singled out)
One of those heavenly days that cannot die;
When, in the eagerness of boyish hope,
I left our cottage-threshold, sallying forth
With a huge wallet o'er my shoulders slung,
A nutting-crook in hand; and turned my steps
Toward some far-distant wood, a Figure quaint,
Tricked out in proud disguise of cast-off weeds
Which for that service had been husbanded,
By exhortation of my frugal Dame—
Motley accoutrement, of power to smile
At thorns, and brakes, and brambles,—and, in truth,
More ragged than need was! O'er pathless rocks,
Through beds of matted fern, and tangled thickets,
Forcing my way, I came to one dear nook
Unvisited, where not a broken bough
Drooped with its withered leaves, ungracious sign
Of devastation; but the hazels rose
Tall and erect, with tempting clusters hung,
A virgin scene!—A little while I stood,
Breathing with such suppression of the heart
As joy delights in; and, with wise restraint
Voluptuous, fearless of a rival, eyed
The banquet;—or beneath the trees I sate
Among the flowers, and with the flowers I played;
A temper known to those who, after long
And weary expectation, have been blest

With sudden happiness beyond all hope.
Perhaps it was a bower beneath whose leaves
The violets of five seasons re-appear
And fade, unseen by any human eye;
Where fairy water-breaks do murmur on
For ever; and I saw the sparkling foam,
And—with my cheek on one of those green stones
That, fleeced with moss, under the shady trees,
Lay round me, scattered like a flock of sheep—
I heard the murmur and the murmuring sound,
In that sweet mood when pleasure loves to pay
Tribute to ease; and, of its joy secure,
The heart luxuriates with indifferent things,
Wasting its kindliness on stocks and stones,
And on the vacant air. Then up I rose,
And dragged to earth both branch and bough, with crash
And merciless ravage: and the shady nook
Of hazels, and the green and mossy bower,
Deformed and sullied, patiently gave up
Their quiet being: and, unless I now
Confound my present feelings with the past,
Ere from the mutilated bower I turned
Exulting, rich beyond the wealth of kings,
I felt a sense of pain when I beheld
The silent trees, and saw the intruding sky.—
Then, dearest Maiden, move along these shades
In gentleness of heart; with gentle hand
Touch—for there is a spirit in the woods.

Lucy Gray; or, Solitude

Oft I had heard of Lucy Gray:
And, when I crossed the wild,
I chanced to see at break of day
The solitary child.

No mate, no comrade Lucy knew;
She dwelt on a wide moor,
—The sweetest thing that ever grew
Beside a human door!

You yet may spy the fawn at play,
The hare upon the green;
But the sweet face of Lucy Gray
Will never more be seen.

'Tonight will be a stormy night—
You to the town must go;
And take a lantern, Child, to light
Your mother through the snow.'

'That, Father! will I gladly do:
'Tis scarcely afternoon—
The minister-clock has just struck two,
And yonder is the moon!'

At this the Father raised his hook,
And snapped a faggot-band;
He plied his work;—and Lucy took
The lantern in her hand.

Not blither is the mountain roe:
With many a wanton stroke

Her feet disperse the powdery snow,
That rises up like smoke.

The storm came on before its time:
She wandered up and down;
And many a hill did Lucy climb:
But never reached the town.

The wretched parents all that night
Went shouting far and wide;
But there was neither sound nor sight
To serve them for a guide.

At day-break on a hill they stood
That overlooked the moor;
And thence they saw the bridge of wood,
A furlong from their door.

They wept—and, turning homeward, cried,
'In heaven we all shall meet';
—When in the snow the mother spied
The print of Lucy's feet.

Then downwards from the steep hill's edge
They tracked the footmarks small;
And through the broken hawthorn hedge,
And by the long stone-wall;

And then an open field they crossed:
The marks were still the same;
They tracked them on, nor ever lost;
And to the bridge they came.

They followed from the snowy bank
Those footmarks, one by one,
Into the middle of the plank;
And further there were none!

—Yet some maintain that to this day
She is a living child;
That you may see sweet Lucy Gray
Upon the lonesome wild.

O'er rough and smooth she trips along,
And never looks behind;
And sings a solitary song
That whistles in the wind.

Fragment: Redundance

Not the more
Failed I to lengthen out my watch. I stood
Within the area of the frozen vale,
Mine eye subdued and quiet as the ear
Of one that listens, for even yet the scene,
Its fluctuating hues and surfaces,
And the decaying vestiges of forms,
Did to the dispossessing power of night
Impart a feeble visionary sense
Of movement and creation doubly felt.

Three years she grew in sun and shower

Three years she grew in sun and shower,
Then Nature said, 'A lovelier flower
On earth was never sown;
This Child I to myself will take;
She shall be mine, and I will make
A Lady of my own.

'Myself will to my darling be
Both law and impulse: and with me
The Girl, in rock and plain,
In earth and heaven, in glade and bower,
Shall feel an overseeing power
To kindle or restrain.

'She shall be sportive as the fawn
That wild with glee across the lawn
Or up the mountain springs;
And hers shall be the breathing balm,
And hers the silence and the calm
Of mute insensate things.

'The floating clouds their state shall lend
To her; for her the willow bend;
Nor shall she fail to see
Even in the motions of the Storm
Grace that shall mould the Maiden's form
By silent sympathy.

'The stars of midnight shall be dear
To her; and she shall lean her ear
In many a secret place
Where rivulets dance their wayward round,

And beauty born of murmuring sound
Shall pass into her face.

'And vital feelings of delight
Shall rear her form to stately height,
Her virgin bosom swell;
Such thoughts to Lucy I will give
While she and I together live
Here in this happy dell.'

Thus Nature spake—The work was done—
How soon my Lucy's race was run!
She died, and left to me
This heath, this calm, and quiet scene;
The memory of what has been,
And never more will be.

A narrow girdle of rough stones and crags

A narrow girdle of rough stones and crags,
A rude and natural causeway, interposed
Between the water and a winding slope
Of copse and thicket, leaves the eastern shore
Of Grasmere safe in its own privacy:
And there myself and two beloved Friends,
One calm September morning, ere the mist
Had altogether yielded to the sun,
Sauntered on this retired and difficult way.
——Ill suits the road with one in haste; but we
Played with our time; and, as we strolled along,
It was our occupation to observe
Such objects as the waves had tossed ashore—
Feather, or leaf, or weed, or withered bough,

Each on the other heaped, along the line
Of the dry wreck. And, in our vacant mood,
Not seldom did we stop to watch some tuft
Of dandelion seed or thistle's beard,
That skimmed the surface of the dead calm lake,
Suddenly halting now—a lifeless stand!
And starting off again with freak as sudden;
In all its sportive wanderings, all the while,
Making report of an invisible breeze
That was its wings, its chariot, and its horse,
Its playmate, rather say, its moving soul.
——And often, trifling with a privilege
Alike indulged to all, we paused, one now,
And now the other, to point out, perchance
To pluck, some flower or water-weed, too fair
Either to be divided from the place
On which it grew, or to be left alone
To its own beauty. Many such there are,
Fair ferns and flowers, and chiefly that tall fern,
So stately, of the Queen Osmunda named;
Plant lovelier, in its own retired abode
On Grasmere's beach, than Naiad by the side
Of Grecian brook, or Lady of the Mere,
Sole-sitting by the shores of old romance.
—So fared we that bright morning: from the fields,
Meanwhile, a noise was heard, the busy mirth
Of reapers, men and women, boys and girls.
Delighted much to listen to those sounds,
And feeding thus our fancies, we advanced
Along the indented shore; when suddenly,
Through a thin veil of glittering haze was seen
Before us, on a point of jutting land,
The tall and upright figure of a Man
Attired in peasant's garb, who stood alone,

Angling beside the margin of the lake.
'Improvident and reckless,' we exclaimed,
'The Man must be, who thus can lose a day
Of the mid harvest, when the labourer's hire
Is ample, and some little might be stored
Wherewith to cheer him in the winter time.'
Thus talking of that Peasant, we approached
Close to the spot where with his rod and line
He stood alone; whereat he turned his head
To greet us—and we saw a Man worn down
By sickness, gaunt and lean, with sunken cheeks
And wasted limbs, his legs so long and lean
That for my single self I looked at them,
Forgetful of the body they sustained.—
Too weak to labour in the harvest field,
The Man was using his best skill to gain
A pittance from the dead unfeeling lake
That knew not of his wants. I will not say
What thoughts immediately were ours, nor how
The happy idleness of that sweet morn,
With all its lovely images, was changed
To serious musing and to self-reproach.
Nor did we fail to see within ourselves
What need there is to be reserved in speech,
And temper all our thoughts with charity.
—Therefore, unwilling to forget that day,
My Friend, Myself, and She who then received
The same admonishment, have called the place
By a memorial name, uncouth indeed
As e'er by mariner was given to bay
Or foreland, on a new-discovered coast;
And POINT RASH-JUDGMENT is the name it bears.

Michael

A PASTORAL POEM

If from the public way you turn your steps
Up the tumultuous brook of Green-head Ghyll,
You will suppose that with an upright path
Your feet must struggle; in such bold ascent
The pastoral mountains front you, face to face.
But, courage! for around that boisterous brook
The mountains have all opened out themselves,
And made a hidden valley of their own.
No habitation can be seen; but they
Who journey thither find themselves alone
With a few sheep, with rocks and stones, and kites
That overhead are sailing in the sky.
It is in truth an utter solitude;
Nor should I have made mention of this Dell
But for one object which you might pass by,
Might see and notice not. Beside the brook
Appears a straggling heap of unhewn stones!
And to that simple object appertains
A story—unenriched with strange events,
Yet not unfit, I deem, for the fireside,
Or for the summer shade. It was the first
Of those domestic tales that spake to me
Of Shepherds, dwellers in the valleys, men
Whom I already loved;—not verily
For their own sakes, but for the fields and hills
Where was their occupation and abode.
And hence this Tale, while I was yet a Boy
Careless of books, yet having felt the power
Of Nature, by the gentle agency
Of natural objects, led me on to feel

For passions that were not my own, and think
(At random and imperfectly indeed)
On man, the heart of man, and human life.
Therefore, although it be a history
Homely and rude, I will relate the same
For the delight of a few natural hearts;
And, with yet fonder feeling, for the sake
Of youthful Poets, who among these hills
Will be my second self when I am gone.

Upon the forest-side in Grasmere Vale
There dwelt a Shepherd, Michael was his name;
An old man, stout of heart, and strong of limb.
His bodily frame had been from youth to age
Of an unusual strength: his mind was keen,
Intense, and frugal, apt for all affairs,
And in his shepherd's calling he was prompt
And watchful more than ordinary men.
Hence had he learned the meaning of all winds,
Of blasts of every tone; and, oftentimes,
When others heeded not, he heard the South
Make subterraneous music, like the noise
Of bagpipers on distant Highland hills.
The Shepherd, at such warning, of his flock
Bethought him, and he to himself would say,
'The winds are now devising work for me!'
And, truly, at all times, the storm, that drives
The traveller to a shelter, summoned him
Up to the mountains: he had been alone
Amid the heart of many thousand mists,
That came to him, and left him, on the heights.
So lived he till his eightieth year was past.
And grossly that man errs, who should suppose
That the green valleys, and the streams and rocks,

Were things indifferent to the Shepherd's thoughts.
Fields, where with cheerful spirits he had breathed
The common air; hills, which with vigorous step
He had so often climbed; which had impressed
So many incidents upon his mind
Of hardship, skill or courage, joy or fear;
Which, like a book, preserved the memory
Of the dumb animals, whom he had saved,
Had fed or sheltered, linking to such acts
The certainty of honourable gain;
Those fields, those hills—what could they less? had laid
Strong hold on his affections, were to him
A pleasurable feeling of blind love,
The pleasure which there is in life itself.

His days had not been passed in singleness.
His Helpmate was a comely matron, old—
Though younger than himself full twenty years.
She was a woman of a stirring life,
Whose heart was in her house: two wheels she had
Of antique form; this large, for spinning wool;
That small, for flax; and if one wheel had rest,
It was because the other was at work.
The Pair had but one inmate in their house,
An only Child, who had been born to them
When Michael, telling o'er his years, began
To deem that he was old,—in shepherd's phrase,
With one foot in the grave. This only Son,
With two brave sheep-dogs tried in many a storm,
The one of an inestimable worth,
Made all their household. I may truly say,
That they were as a proverb in the vale
For endless industry. When day was gone,
And from their occupations out of doors

The Son and Father were come home, even then,
Their labour did not cease; unless when all
Turned to the cleanly supper-board, and there,
Each with a mess of pottage and skimmed milk,
Sat round the basket piled with oaten cakes,
And their plain home-made cheese. Yet when the meal
Was ended, Luke (for so the Son was named)
And his old Father both betook themselves
To such convenient work as might employ
Their hands by the fire-side; perhaps to card
Wool for the Housewife's spindle, or repair
Some injury done to sickle, flail, or scythe,
Or other implement of house or field.

    Down from the ceiling, by the chimney's edge,
That in our ancient uncouth country style
With huge and black projection overbrowed
Large space beneath, as duly as the light
Of day grew dim the Housewife hung a lamp;
An aged utensil, which had performed
Service beyond all others of its kind.
Early at evening did it burn—and late,
Surviving comrade of uncounted hours,
Which, going by from year to year, had found,
And left the couple neither gay perhaps
Nor cheerful, yet with objects and with hopes,
Living a life of eager industry.
And now, when Luke had reached his eighteenth year,
There by the light of this old lamp they sate,
Father and Son, while far into the night
The Housewife plied her own peculiar work,
Making the cottage through the silent hours
Murmur as with the sound of summer flies.
This light was famous in its neighbourhood,

And was a public symbol of the life
That thrifty Pair had lived. For, as it chanced,
Their cottage on a plot of rising ground
Stood single, with large prospect, north and south,
High into Easedale, up to Dunmail-Raise,
And westward to the village near the lake;
And from this constant light, so regular
And so far seen, the House itself, by all
Who dwelt within the limits of the vale,
Both old and young, was named THE EVENING STAR.

Thus living on through such a length of years,
The Shepherd, if he loved himself, must needs
Have loved his Helpmate; but to Michael's heart
This son of his old age was yet more dear—
Less from instinctive tenderness, the same
Fond spirit that blindly works in the blood of all—
Than that a child, more than all other gifts
That earth can offer to declining man,
Brings hope with it, and forward-looking thoughts,
And stirrings of inquietude, when they
By tendency of nature needs must fail.
Exceeding was the love he bare to him,
His heart and his heart's joy! For often-times
Old Michael, while he was a babe in arms,
Had done him female service, not alone
For pastime and delight, as is the use
Of fathers, but with patient mind enforced
To acts of tenderness; and he had rocked
His cradle, as with a woman's gentle hand.

And, in a later time, ere yet the Boy
Had put on boy's attire, did Michael love,
Albeit of a stern unbending mind,

To have the Young-one in his sight, when he
Wrought in the field, or on his shepherd's stool
Sate with a fettered sheep before him stretched
Under the large old oak, that near his door
Stood single, and, from matchless depth of shade,
Chosen for the Shearer's covert from the sun,
Thence in our rustic dialect was called
The CLIPPING TREE, a name which yet it bears.
There, while they two were sitting in the shade,
With others round them, earnest all and blithe,
Would Michael exercise his heart with looks
Of fond correction and reproof bestowed
Upon the Child, if he disturbed the sheep
By catching at their legs, or with his shouts
Scared them, while they lay still beneath the shears.

And when by Heaven's good grace the boy grew up
A healthy Lad, and carried in his cheek
Two steady roses that were five years old;
Then Michael from a winter coppice cut
With his own hand a sapling, which he hooped
With iron, making it throughout in all
Due requisites a perfect shepherd's staff,
And gave it to the Boy; wherewith equipt
He as a watchman oftentimes was placed
At gate or gap, to stem or turn the flock;
And, to his office prematurely called,
There stood the urchin, as you will divine,
Something between a hindrance and a help;
And for this cause not always, I believe,
Receiving from his Father hire of praise;
Though naught was left undone which staff, or voice,
Or looks, or threatening gestures, could perform.

But soon as Luke, full ten years old, could stand
Against the mountain blasts; and to the heights,
Not fearing toil, nor length of weary ways,
He with his Father daily went, and they
Were as companions, why should I relate
That objects which the Shepherd loved before
Were dearer now? that from the Boy there came
Feelings and emanations—things which were
Light to the sun and music to the wind;
And that the old Man's heart seemed born again?

Thus in his Father's sight the Boy grew up:
And now, when he had reached his eighteenth year,
He was his comfort and his daily hope.

While in this sort the simple household lived
From day to day, to Michael's ear there came
Distressful tidings. Long before the time
Of which I speak, the Shepherd had been bound
In surety for his brother's son, a man
Of an industrious life, and ample means;
But unforeseen misfortunes suddenly
Had prest upon him; and old Michael now
Was summoned to discharge the forfeiture,
A grievous penalty, but little less
Than half his substance. This unlooked-for claim,
At the first hearing, for a moment took
More hope out of his life than he supposed
That any old man ever could have lost.
As soon as he had armed himself with strength
To look his trouble in the face, it seemed
The Shepherd's sole resource to sell at once
A portion of his patrimonial fields.
Such was his first resolve; he thought again,

And his heart failed him. 'Isabel,' said he,
Two evenings after he had heard the news,
'I have been toiling more than seventy years,
And in the open sunshine of God's love
Have we all lived; yet if these fields of ours
Should pass into a stranger's hand, I think
That I could not lie quiet in my grave.
Our lot is a hard lot; the sun himself
Has scarcely been more diligent than I;
And I have lived to be a fool at last
To my own family. An evil man
That was, and made an evil choice, if he
Were false to us; and if he were not false,
There are ten thousand to whom loss like this
Had been no sorrow. I forgive him;—but
'Twere better to be dumb than to talk thus.

'When I began, my purpose was to speak
Of remedies and of a cheerful hope.
Our Luke shall leave us, Isabel; the land
Shall not go from us, and it shall be free;
He shall possess it, free as is the wind
That passes over it. We have, thou know'st,
Another kinsman—he will be our friend
In this distress. He is a prosperous man,
Thriving in trade—and Luke to him shall go,
And with his kinsman's help and his own thrift
He quickly will repair this loss, and then
He may return to us. If here he stay,
What can be done? Where every one is poor,
What can be gained?'
                          At this the old Man paused,
And Isabel sat silent, for her mind
Was busy, looking back into past times.

There's Richard Bateman, thought she to herself,
He was a parish-boy—at the church-door
They made a gathering for him, shillings, pence,
And halfpennies, wherewith the neighbours bought
A basket, which they filled with pedlar's wares;
And, with this basket on his arm, the lad
Went up to London, found a master there,
Who, out of many, chose the trusty boy
To go and overlook his merchandise
Beyond the seas; where he grew wondrous rich,
And left estates and monies to the poor,
And, at his birth-place, built a chapel floored
With marble, which he sent from foreign lands.
These thoughts, and many others of like sort,
Passed quickly through the mind of Isabel,
And her face brightened. The old Man was glad,
And thus resumed:—'Well, Isabel! this scheme
These two days, has been meat and drink to me.
Far more than we have lost is left us yet.
—We have enough—I wish indeed that I
Were younger;—but this hope is a good hope.
Make ready Luke's best garments, of the best
Buy for him more, and let us send him forth
Tomorrow, or the next day, or tonight:
—If he *could* go, the Boy should go tonight.'

Here Michael ceased, and to the fields went forth
With a light heart. The Housewife for five days
Was restless morn and night and all day long
Wrought on with her best fingers to prepare
Things needful for the journey of her son.
But Isabel was glad when Sunday came
To stop her in her work: for, when she lay
By Michael's side, she through the last two nights

Heard him, how he was troubled in his sleep:
And when they rose at morning she could see
That all his hopes were gone. That day at noon
She said to Luke, while they two by themselves
Were sitting at the door, 'Thou must not go:
We have no other Child but thee to lose,
None to remember—do not go away,
For if thou leave thy Father he will die.'
The Youth made answer with a jocund voice;
And Isabel, when she had told her fears,
Recovered heart. That evening her best fare
Did she bring forth, and all together sat
Like happy people round a Christmas fire.

    With daylight Isabel resumed her work;
And all the ensuing week the house appeared
As cheerful as a grove in Spring: at length
The expected letter from their kinsman came,
With kind assurances that he would do
His utmost for the welfare of the Boy;
To which, requests were added, that forthwith
He might be sent to him. Ten times or more
The letter was read over; Isabel
Went forth to show it to the neighbours round;
Nor was there at that time on English land
A prouder heart than Luke's. When Isabel
Had to her house returned, the old Man said,
'He shall depart tomorrow.' To this word
The Housewife answered, talking much of things
Which, if at such short notice he should go,
Would surely be forgotten. But at length
She gave consent, and Michael was at ease.

Near the tumultuous brook of Green-head Ghyll,
In that deep valley, Michael had designed
To build a Sheep-fold; and, before he heard
The tidings of his melancholy loss,
For this same purpose he had gathered up
A heap of stones, which by the streamlet's edge
Lay thrown together, ready for the work.
With Luke that evening thitherward he walked:
And soon as they had reached the place he stopped,
And thus the old Man spake to him:—'My Son,
Tomorrow thou wilt leave me: with full heart
I look upon thee, for thou art the same
That wert a promise to me ere thy birth,
And all thy life hast been my daily joy.
I will relate to thee some little part
Of our two histories; 'twill do thee good
When thou art from me, even if I should touch
On things thou canst not know of.—After thou
First cam'st into the world—as oft befalls
To new-born infants—thou didst sleep away
Two days, and blessings from thy Father's tongue
Then fell upon thee. Day by day passed on,
And still I loved thee with increasing love.
Never to living ear came sweeter sounds
Than when I heard thee by our own fire-side
First uttering, without words, a natural tune;
While thou, a feeding babe, didst in thy joy
Sing at thy Mother's breast. Month followed month,
And in the open fields my life was passed
And on the mountains; else I think that thou
Hadst been brought up upon thy Father's knees.
But we were playmates, Luke: among these hills,
As well thou knowest, in us the old and young

Have played together, nor with me didst thou
Lack any pleasure which a boy can know.'
Luke had a manly heart; but at these words
He sobbed aloud. The old Man grasped his hand,
And said, 'Nay, do not take it so—I see
That these are things of which I need not speak.
—Even to the utmost I have been to thee
A kind and a good Father: and herein
I but repay a gift which I myself
Received at others' hands; for, though now old
Beyond the common life of man, I still
Remember them who loved me in my youth.
Both of them sleep together: here they lived,
As all their Forefathers had done; and when
At length their time was come, they were not loth
To give their bodies to the family mould.
I wished that thou should'st live the life they lived:
But 'tis a long time to look back, my Son,
And see so little gain from threescore years.
These fields were burdened when they came to me;
Till I was forty years of age, not more
Than half of my inheritance was mine.
I toiled and toiled; God blessed me in my work,
And till these three weeks past the land was free.
—It looks as if it never could endure
Another Master. Heaven forgive me, Luke,
If I judge ill for thee, but it seems good
That thou shouldst go.'
                              At this the old Man paused;
Then, pointing to the stones near which they stood,
Thus, after a short silence, he resumed:
'This was a work for us; and now, my Son,
It is a work for me. But, lay one stone—
Here, lay it for me, Luke, with thine own hands.

Nay, Boy, be of good hope;—we both may live
To see a better day. At eighty-four
I still am strong and hale;—do thou thy part;
I will do mine.—I will begin again
With many tasks that were resigned to thee:
Up to the heights, and in among the storms,
Will I without thee go again, and do
All works which I was wont to do alone,
Before I knew thy face.—Heaven bless thee, Boy!
Thy heart these two weeks has been beating fast
With many hopes; it should be so—yes—yes—
I knew that thou couldst never have a wish
To leave me, Luke: thou hast been bound to me
Only by links of love: when thou art gone,
What will be left to us!—But, I forget
My purposes. Lay now the corner-stone,
As I requested; and hereafter, Luke,
When thou art gone away, should evil men
Be thy companions, think of me, my Son,
And of this moment; hither turn thy thoughts,
And God will strengthen thee: amid all fear
And all temptation, Luke, I pray that thou
May'st bear in mind the life thy Fathers lived,
Who, being innocent, did for that cause
Bestir them in good deeds. Now, fare thee well—
When thou return'st, thou in this place wilt see
A work which is not here: a covenant
'Twill be between us; but, whatever fate
Befall thee, I shall love thee to the last,
And bear thy memory with me to the grave.'

The Shepherd ended here; and Luke stooped down,
And, as his Father had requested, laid
The first stone of the Sheep-fold. At the sight

The old Man's grief broke from him; to his heart
He pressed his Son, he kissèd him and wept;
And to the house together they returned.
—Hushed was that House in peace, or seeming peace,
Ere the night fell:—with morrow's dawn the Boy
Began his journey, and when he had reached
The public way, he put on a bold face;
And all the neighbours, as he passed their doors,
Came forth with wishes and with farewell prayers,
That followed him till he was out of sight.

A good report did from their Kinsman come,
Of Luke and his well-doing: and the Boy
Wrote loving letters, full of wondrous news,
Which, as the Housewife phrased it, were throughout
'The prettiest letters that were ever seen.'
Both parents read them with rejoicing hearts.
So, many months passed on: and once again
The Shepherd went about his daily work
With confident and cheerful thoughts; and now
Sometimes when he could find a leisure hour
He to that valley took his way, and there
Wrought at the Sheep-fold. Meantime Luke began
To slacken in his duty; and, at length,
He in the dissolute city gave himself
To evil courses: ignominy and shame
Fell on him, so that he was driven at last
To seek a hiding-place beyond the seas.

There is a comfort in the strength of love;
'Twill make a thing endurable, which else
Would overset the brain, or break the heart:
I have conversed with more than one who well

Remember the old Man, and what he was
Years after he had heard this heavy news.
His bodily frame had been from youth to age
Of an unusual strength. Among the rocks
He went, and still looked up to sun and cloud,
And listened to the wind; and, as before,
Performed all kinds of labour for his sheep,
And for the land, his small inheritance.
And to that hollow dell from time to time
Did he repair, to build the Fold of which
His flock had need. 'Tis not forgotten yet
The pity which was then in every heart
For the old Man—and 'tis believed by all
That many and many a day he thither went,
And never lifted up a single stone.

There, by the Sheep-fold, sometimes was he seen
Sitting alone, or with his faithful Dog,
Then old, beside him, lying at his feet.
The length of full seven years, from time to time,
He at the building of this Sheep-fold wrought,
And left the work unfinished when he died.
Three years, or little more, did Isabel
Survive her Husband: at her death the estate
Was sold, and went into a stranger's hand.
The Cottage which was named the EVENING STAR
Is gone—the ploughshare has been through the ground
On which it stood; great changes have been wrought
In all the neighbourhood:—yet the oak is left
That grew beside their door; and the remains
Of the unfinished Sheep-fold may be seen
Beside the boisterous brook of Green-head Ghyll.

from *Preface to* Lyrical Ballads, with Pastoral and Other Poems *(1802)*

The first Volume of these Poems has already been submitted to general perusal. It was published, as an experiment, which, I hoped, might be of some use to ascertain, how far, by fitting to metrical arrangement a selection of the real language of men in a state of vivid sensation, that sort of pleasure and that quantity of pleasure may be imparted, which a Poet may rationally endeavour to impart.

I had formed no very inaccurate estimate of the probable effect of those Poems: I flattered myself that they who should be pleased with them would read them with more than common pleasure: and, on the other hand, I was well aware, that by those who should dislike them they would be read with more than common dislike. The result has differed from my expectation in this only, that I have pleased a greater number, than I ventured to hope I should please. . . .

Several of my Friends are anxious for the success of these Poems from a belief, that, if the views with which they were composed were indeed realized, a class of Poetry would be produced, well adapted to interest mankind permanently, and not unimportant in the multiplicity, and in the quality of its moral relations: and on this account they have advised me to prefix a systematic defence of the theory upon which the poems were written. But I was unwilling to undertake the task, because I knew that on this occasion the Reader would look coldly upon my arguments, since I might be suspected of having been principally influenced by the selfish and foolish hope of *reasoning* him into an approbation of these particular Poems: and I was still more unwilling to undertake the task, because, adequately to display my opinions, and fully to enforce my arguments, would require a space wholly disproportionate to the nature of a preface. For to treat the subject with the clearness and coherence, of which I believe it susceptible, it would be necessary to give a full account of the present state of the public taste in this country, and to determine how far this taste is healthy or depraved; which, again, could not be determined, without pointing out, in what manner language and

the human mind act and re-act on each other, and without retracing the revolutions, not of literature alone, but likewise of society itself. I have therefore altogether declined to enter regularly upon this defence; yet I am sensible, that there would be some impropriety in abruptly obtruding upon the Public, without a few words of introduction, Poems so materially different from those upon which general approbation is at present bestowed.

It is supposed, that by the act of writing in verse an Author makes a formal engagement that he will gratify certain known habits of association; that he not only thus apprises the Reader that certain classes of ideas and expressions will be found in his book, but that others will be carefully excluded. This exponent or symbol held forth by metrical language must in different eras of literature have excited very different expectations: for example, in the age of Catullus, Terence, and Lucretius, and that of Statius or Claudian; and in our own country, in the age of Shakespeare and Beaumont and Fletcher, and that of Donne and Cowley, or Dryden, or Pope. I will not take upon me to determine the exact import of the promise which by the act of writing in verse an Author, in the present day, makes to his Reader; but I am certain, it will appear to many persons that I have not fulfilled the terms of an engagement thus voluntarily contracted. They who have been accustomed to the gaudiness and inane phraseology of many modern writers, if they persist in reading this book to its conclusion, will, no doubt, frequently have to struggle with feelings of strangeness and awkwardness: they will look round for poetry, and will be induced to inquire by what species of courtesy these attempts can be permitted to assume that title. I hope therefore the Reader will not censure me, if I attempt to state what I have proposed to myself to perform; and also (as far as the limits of a preface will permit) to explain some of the chief reasons which have determined me in the choice of my purpose: that at least he may be spared any unpleasant feeling of disappointment, and that I myself may be protected from the most dishonourable accusation which can be brought against an Author, namely, that of an indolence which prevents him from en-

deavouring to ascertain what is his duty, or, when his duty is ascertained, prevents him from performing it.

The principal object, then, which I proposed to myself in these Poems was to choose incidents and situations from common life, and to relate or describe them, throughout, as far as was possible, in a selection of language really used by men; and, at the same time, to throw over them a certain colouring of imagination, whereby ordinary things should be presented to the mind in an unusual way; and, further, and above all, to make these incidents and situations interesting by tracing in them, truly though not ostentatiously, the primary laws of our nature: chiefly, as far as regards the manner in which we associate ideas in a state of excitement. Low and rustic life was generally chosen, because in that condition, the essential passions of the heart find a better soil in which they can attain their maturity, are less under restraint, and speak a plainer and more emphatic language; because in that condition of life our elementary feelings co-exist in a state of greater simplicity, and, consequently, may be more accurately contemplated, and more forcibly communicated; because the manners of rural life germinate from those elementary feelings; and, from the necessary character of rural occupations, are more easily comprehended; and are more durable; and lastly, because in that condition the passions of men are incorporated with the beautiful and permanent forms of nature. The language, too, of these men is adopted (purified indeed from what appear to be its real defects, from all lasting and rational causes of dislike or disgust) because such men hourly communicate with the best objects from which the best part of language is originally derived; and because, from their rank in society and the sameness and narrow circle of their intercourse, being less under the influence of social vanity, they convey their feelings and notions in simple and unelaborated expressions. Accordingly, such a language, arising out of repeated experience and regular feelings, is a more permanent, and a far more philosophical language, than that which is frequently substituted for it by Poets, who think that they are conferring honour upon themselves and their art, in proportion as they separate themselves from the sympathies of men, and indulge in arbitrary and

capricious habits of expression, in order to furnish food for fickle tastes, and fickle appetites, of their own creation. [It is worthwhile here to observe that the affecting parts of Chaucer are almost always expressed in language pure and universally intelligible even to this day.—W.]

I cannot, however, be insensible of the present outcry against the triviality and meanness both of thought and language, which some of my contemporaries have occasionally introduced into their metrical compositions; and I acknowledge that this defect, where it exists, is more dishonourable to the Writer's own character than false refinement or arbitrary innovation, though I should contend at the same time that it is far less pernicious in the sum of its consequences. From such verses the Poems in these volumes will be found distinguished at least by one mark of difference, that each of them has a worthy *purpose*. Not that I mean to say, that I always began to write with a distinct purpose formally conceived; but I believe that my habits of meditation have so formed my feelings, as that my descriptions of such objects as strongly excite those feelings, will be found to carry along with them a *purpose*. If in this opinion I am mistaken, I can have little right to the name of a Poet. For all good poetry is the spontaneous overflow of powerful feelings: but though this be true, Poems to which any value can be attached, were never produced on any variety of subjects but by a man, who being possessed of more than usual organic sensibility, had also thought long and deeply. For our continued influxes of feeling are modified and directed by our thoughts, which are indeed the representatives of all our past feelings; and, as by contemplating the relation of these general representatives to each other we discover what is really important to men, so, by the repetition and continuance of this act, our feelings will be connected with important subjects, till at length, if we be originally possessed of much sensibility, such habits of mind will be produced, that, by obeying blindly and mechanically the impulses of those habits, we shall describe objects, and utter sentiments, of such a nature and in such connexion with each other, that the understanding of the being to whom we address ourselves, if he be in a healthful state of association,

must necessarily be in some degree enlightened, and his affections ameliorated. . . .

I will not suffer a sense of false modesty to prevent me from asserting, that I point my Reader's attention to this mark of distinction, far less for the sake of these particular Poems than from the general importance of the subject. The subject is indeed important! For the human mind is capable of being excited without the application of gross and violent stimulants; and he must have a very faint perception of its beauty and dignity who does not know this, and who does not further know, that one being is elevated above another, in proportion as he possesses this capability. It has therefore appeared to me, that to endeavour to produce or enlarge this capability is one of the best services in which, at any period, a Writer can be engaged; but this service, excellent at all times, is especially so at the present day. For a multitude of causes, unknown to former times, are now acting with a combined force to blunt the discriminating powers of the mind, and unfitting it for all voluntary exertion to reduce it to a state of almost savage torpor. The most effective of these causes are the great national events which are daily taking place, and the increasing accumulation of men in cities, where the uniformity of their occupations produces a craving for extraordinary incident, which the rapid communication of intelligence hourly gratifies. To this tendency of life and manners the literature and theatrical exhibitions of the country have conformed themselves. The invaluable works of our elder writers, I had almost said the works of Shakespeare and Milton, are driven into neglect by frantic novels, sickly and stupid German Tragedies, and deluges of idle and extravagant stories in verse.—When I think upon this degrading thirst after outrageous stimulation, I am almost ashamed to have spoken of the feeble effort with which I have endeavoured to counteract it; and, reflecting upon the magnitude of the general evil, I should be oppressed with no dishonourable melancholy, had I not a deep impression of certain inherent and indestructible qualities of the human mind, and likewise of certain powers in the great and permanent objects that act upon it, which are equally inherent and indestructible; and did I not further add to this

impression a belief, that the time is approaching when the evil will be systematically opposed, by men of greater powers, and with far more distinguished success.

Having dwelt thus long on the subjects and aim of these Poems, I shall request the Reader's permission to apprise him of a few circumstances relating to their *style,* in order, among other reasons, that I may not be censured for not having performed what I never attempted. The Reader will find that personifications of abstract ideas rarely occur in these volumes; and, I hope, are utterly rejected as an ordinary device to elevate the style, and raise it above prose. I have proposed to myself to imitate, and, as far as is possible, to adopt the very language of men; and assuredly such personifications do not make any natural or regular part of that language. They are, indeed, a figure of speech occasionally prompted by passion, and I have made use of them as such; but I have endeavoured utterly to reject them as a mechanical device of style, or as a family language which Writers in metre seem to lay claim to by prescription. I have wished to keep my Reader in the company of flesh and blood, persuaded that by so doing I shall interest him. I am, however, well aware that others who pursue a different track may interest him likewise; I do not interfere with their claim, I only wish to prefer a different claim of my own. There will also be found in these volumes little of what is usually called poetic diction; I have taken as much pains to avoid it as others ordinarily take to produce it; this I have done for the reason already alleged, to bring my language near to the language of men, and further, because the pleasure which I have proposed to myself to impart is of a kind very different from that which is supposed by many persons to be the proper object of poetry. . . .

Taking up the subject, then, upon general grounds, I ask what is meant by the word Poet? What is a Poet? To whom does he address himself? And what language is to be expected from him? He is a man speaking to men: a man, it is true, endued with more lively sensibility, more enthusiasm and tenderness, who has a greater knowledge of human nature, and a more comprehensive soul, than are supposed to be common among mankind; a man pleased with his own passions and voli-

tions, and who rejoices more than other men in the spirit of life that is in him; delighting to contemplate similar volitions and passions as manifested in the goings-on of the Universe, and habitually impelled to create them where he does not find them. To these qualities he has added a disposition to be affected more than other men by absent things as if they were present; an ability of conjuring up in himself passions, which are indeed far from being the same as those produced by real events, yet (especially in those parts of the general sympathy which are pleasing and delightful) do more nearly resemble the passions produced by real events, than anything which, from the motions of their own minds merely, other men are accustomed to feel in themselves; whence, and from practise, he has acquired a greater readiness and power in expressing what he thinks and feels, and especially those thoughts and feelings which, by his own choice, or from the structure of his own mind, arise in him without immediate external excitement. . . .

Aristotle, I have been told, hath said, that Poetry is the most philosophic of all writing: it is so: its object is truth, not individual and local, but general, and operative; not standing upon external testimony, but carried alive into the heart by passion; truth which is its own testimony, which gives strength and divinity to the tribunal to which it appeals, and receives them from the same tribunal. Poetry is the image of man and nature. The obstacles which stand in the way of the fidelity of the Biographer and Historian, and of their consequent utility, are incalculably greater than those which are to be encountered by the Poet who has an adequate notion of the dignity of his art. The Poet writes under one restriction only, namely, that of the necessity of giving immediate pleasure to a human Being possessed of that information which may be expected from him, not as a lawyer, a physician, a mariner, an astronomer or a natural philosopher, but as a Man. Except this one restriction, there is no object standing between the Poet and the image of things; between this, and the Biographer and Historian there are a thousand.

Nor let this necessity of producing immediate pleasure be considered as a degradation of the Poet's art. It is far otherwise. It is an acknowledgement of the beauty of the universe, an acknowledgement the more

sincere, because it is not formal, but indirect; it is a task light and easy to him who looks at the world in the spirit of love: further, it is a homage paid to the native and naked dignity of man, to the grand elementary principle of pleasure, by which he knows, and feels, and lives, and moves. We have no sympathy but what is propagated by pleasure: I would not be misunderstood; but wherever we sympathize with pain it will be found that the sympathy is produced and carried on by subtle combinations with pleasure. We have no knowledge, that is, no general principles drawn from the contemplation of particular facts, but what has been built up by pleasure, and exists in us by pleasure alone. The Man of Science, the Chemist and Mathematician, whatever difficulties and disgusts they may have had to struggle with, know and feel this. However painful may be the objects with which the Anatomist's knowledge is connected, he feels that his knowledge is pleasure; and where he has no pleasure he has no knowledge. What then does the Poet? He considers man and the objects that surround him as acting and re-acting upon each other, so as to produce an infinite complexity of pain and pleasure; he considers man in his own nature and in his ordinary life as contemplating this with a certain quantity of immediate knowledge, with certain convictions, intuitions, and deductions which by habit become of the nature of intuitions; he considers him as looking upon this complex scene of ideas and sensations, and finding everywhere objects that immediately excite in him sympathies which, from the necessities of his nature, are accompanied by an overbalance of enjoyment.

To this knowledge which all men carry about with them, and to these sympathies in which without any other discipline than that of our daily life we are fitted to take delight, the Poet principally directs his attention. He considers man and nature as essentially adapted to each other, and the mind of man as naturally the mirror of the fairest and most interesting qualities of nature. And thus the Poet, prompted by this feeling of pleasure which accompanies him through the whole course of his studies, converses with general nature with affections akin to those, which, through labour and length of time, the Man of Science

has raised up in himself, by conversing with those particular parts of nature which are the objects of his studies. The knowledge both of the Poet and the Man of Science is pleasure; but the knowledge of the one cleaves to us as a necessary part of our existence, our natural and unalienable inheritance; the other is a personal and individual acquisition, slow to come to us, and by no habitual and direct sympathy connecting us with our fellow-beings. The Man of Science seeks truth as a remote and unknown benefactor; he cherishes and loves it in his solitude: the Poet, singing a song in which all human beings join with him, rejoices in the presence of truth as our visible friend and hourly companion. Poetry is the breath and finer spirit of all knowledge; it is the impassioned expression which is in the countenance of all Science. Emphatically may it be said of the Poet, as Shakespeare hath said of man, 'that he looks before and after.' He is the rock of defence of human nature; an upholder and preserver, carrying everywhere with him relationship and love. In spite of difference of soil and climate, of language and manners, of laws and customs, in spite of things silently gone out of mind and things violently destroyed, the Poet binds together by passion and knowledge the vast empire of human society, as it is spread over the whole earth, and over all time. The objects of the Poet's thoughts are everywhere; though the eyes and senses of man are, it is true, his favourite guides, yet he will follow wheresoever he can find an atmosphere of sensation in which to move his wings. Poetry is the first and last of all knowledge—it is as immortal as the heart of man. If the labours of Men of Science should ever create any material revolution, direct or indirect, in our condition, and in the impressions which we habitually receive, the Poet will sleep then no more than at present, but he will be ready to follow the steps of the Man of Science, not only in those general indirect effects, but he will be at his side, carrying sensation into the midst of the objects of the Science itself. The remotest discoveries of the Chemist, the Botanist, or Mineralogist, will be as proper objects of the Poet's art as any upon which it can be employed, if the time should ever come when these things shall be familiar to us, and the relations under which they are contemplated by

the followers of these respective Sciences shall be manifestly and palpably material to us as enjoying and suffering beings. If the time should ever come when what is now called Science, thus familiarized to men, shall be ready to put on, as it were, a form of flesh and blood, the Poet will lend his divine spirit to aid the transfiguration, and will welcome the Being thus produced, as a dear and genuine inmate of the household of man.—It is not, then, to be supposed that anyone, who holds that sublime notion of Poetry which I have attempted to convey, will break in upon the sanctity and truth of his pictures by transitory and accidental ornaments, and endeavour to excite admiration of himself by arts, the necessity of which must manifestly depend upon the assumed meanness of his subject. . . .

If I had undertaken a systematic defence of the theory upon which these poems are written, it would have been my duty to develope the various causes upon which the pleasure received from metrical language depends. Among the chief of these causes is to be reckoned a principle which must be well known to those who have made any of the Arts the object of accurate reflection; I mean the pleasure which the mind derives from the perception of similitude in dissimilitude. This principle is the great spring of the activity of our minds, and their chief feeder. From this principle the direction of the sexual appetite, and all the passions connected with it, take their origin: it is the life of our ordinary conversation; and upon the accuracy with which similitude in dissimilitude, and dissimilitude in similitude are perceived, depend our taste and our moral feelings. It would not have been a useless employment to have applied this principle to the consideration of metre, and to have shown that metre is hence enabled to afford much pleasure, and to have pointed out in what manner that pleasure is produced. But my limits will not permit me to enter upon this subject, and I must content myself with a general summary.

I have said that Poetry is the spontaneous overflow of powerful feelings: it takes its origin from emotion recollected in tranquillity: the emotion is contemplated till by a species of reaction the tranquillity gradually disappears, and an emotion, kindred to that which was before

the subject of contemplation, is gradually produced, and does itself
actually exist in the mind. In this mood successful composition generally
begins, and in a mood similar to this it is carried on; but the emotion,
of whatever kind and in whatever degree, from various causes is quali-
fied by various pleasures, so that in describing any passions whatsoever,
which are voluntarily described, the mind will upon the whole be in
a state of enjoyment. Now, if Nature be thus cautious in preserving in
a state of enjoyment a being thus employed, the Poet ought to profit
by the lesson thus held forth to him, and ought especially to take care,
that whatever passions he communicates to his Reader, those passions,
if his Reader's mind be sound and vigorous, should always be accom-
panied with an overbalance of pleasure. Now the music of harmonious
metrical language, the sense of difficulty overcome, and the blind associ-
ation of pleasure which has been previously received from works of
rhyme or metre of the same or similar construction, an indistinct
perception perpetually renewed of language closely resembling that of
real life, and yet, in the circumstance of metre, differing from it so
widely—all these imperceptibly make up a complex feeling of delight,
which is of the most important use in tempering the painful feeling
which will always be found intermingled with powerful descriptions
of the deeper passions. This effect is always produced in pathetic and
impassioned poetry; while, in lighter compositions, the ease and grace-
fulness with which the Poet manages his numbers are themselves con-
fessedly a principal source of the gratification of the Reader. I might
perhaps include all which it is *necessary* to say upon this subject by
affirming, what few persons will deny, that, of two descriptions, either
of passions, manners, or characters, each of them equally well executed,
the one in prose and the other in verse, the verse will be read a hundred
times where the prose is read once. We see that Pope, by the power of
verse alone, has contrived to render the plainest common sense interest-
ing, and even frequently to invest it with the appearance of passion. In
consequence of these convictions I related in metre the Tale of GOODY
BLAKE AND HARRY GILL, which is one of the rudest of this collection. I
wished to draw attention to the truth, that the power of the human

imagination is sufficient to produce such changes even in our physical nature as might almost appear miraculous. The truth is an important one; the fact (for it is a *fact*) is a valuable illustration of it. And I have the satisfaction of knowing that it has been communicated to many hundreds of people who would never have heard of it, had it not been narrated as a Ballad, and in a more impressive metre than is usual in Ballads. . . .

I have one request to make of my Reader, which is, that in judging these Poems he would decide by his own feelings genuinely, and not by reflection upon what will probably be the judgement of others. How common is it to hear a person say, 'I myself do not object to this style of composition, or this or that expression, but to such and such classes of people it will appear mean or ludicrous.' This mode of criticism, so destructive of all sound unadulterated judgement, is almost universal: I have therefore to request, that the Reader would abide independently by his own feelings, and that if he finds himself affected he would not suffer such conjectures to interfere with his pleasure. . . .

The Two-Part Prelude

FIRST PART

Was it for this
That one, the fairest of all rivers, loved
To blend his murmurs with my nurse's song,
And from his alder shades and rocky falls,
And from his fords and shallows, sent a voice
That flowed along my dreams? For this didst thou,
O Derwent, travelling over the green plains
Near my 'sweet birthplace', didst thou, beauteous stream,
Make ceaseless music through the night and day,
Which with its steady cadence tempering
Our human waywardness, composed my thoughts

To more than infant softness, giving me
Among the fretful dwellings of mankind
A knowledge, a dim earnest, of the calm
Which Nature breathes among the fields and groves?
Beloved Derwent, fairest of all streams,
Was it for this that I, a four years' child,
A naked boy, among thy silent pools
Made one long bathing of a summer's day,
Basked in the sun, or plunged into thy streams,
Alternate, all a summer's day, or coursed
Over the sandy fields, and dashed the flowers
Of yellow grunsel; or, when crag and hill,
The woods, and distant Skiddaw's lofty height,
Were bronzed with a deep radiance, stood alone
A naked savage in the thunder-shower?
    And afterwards ('twas in a later day,
Though early), when upon the mountain slope
The frost and breath of frosty wind had snapped
The last autumnal crocus, 'twas my joy
To wander half the night among the cliffs
And the smooth hollows where the woodcocks ran
Along the moonlight turf. In thought and wish
That time, my shoulder all with springes hung,
I was a fell destroyer. Gentle powers,
Who give us happiness and call it peace,
When scudding on from snare to snare I plied
My anxious visitation, hurrying on,
Still hurrying, hurrying onward, how my heart
Panted!—among the scattered yew-trees and the crags
That looked upon me, how my bosom beat
With expectation! Sometimes strong desire
Resistless overpowered me, and the bird
Which was the captive of another's toils

Became my prey; and when the deed was done
I heard among the solitary hills
Low breathings coming after me, and sounds
Of undistinguishable motion, steps
Almost as silent as the turf they trod.

    Nor less in springtime, when on southern banks
The shining sun had from his knot of leaves
Decoyed the primrose flower, and when the vales
And woods were warm, was I a rover then
In the high places, on the lonesome peaks,
Among the mountains and the winds. Though mean
And though inglorious were my views, the end
Was not ignoble. Oh, when I have hung
Above the raven's nest, by knots of grass
Or half-inch fissures in the slippery rock
But ill sustained, and almost, as it seemed,
Suspended by the blast which blew amain,
Shouldering the naked crag, oh, at that time,
While on the perilous ridge I hung alone,
With what strange utterance did the loud dry wind
Blow through my ears; the sky seemed not a sky
Of earth, and with what motion moved the clouds!

    The mind of man is fashioned and built up
Even as a strain of music. I believe
That there are spirits which, when they would form
A favored being, from his very dawn
Of infancy do open out the clouds
As at the touch of lightning, seeking him
With gentle visitation—quiet powers,
Retired, and seldom recognized, yet kind,
And to the very meanest not unknown—
With me, though rarely, in my boyish days
They communed. Others too there are, who use,

Yet haply aiming at the self-same end,
Severer interventions, ministry
More palpable—and of their school was I.
    They guided me: one evening led by them
I went alone into a shepherd's boat,
A skiff, that to a willow-tree was tied
Within a rocky cave, its usual home.
The moon was up, the lake was shining clear
Among the hoary mountains; from the shore
I pushed, and struck the oars, and struck again
In cadence, and my little boat moved on
Just like a man who walks with stately step
Though bent on speed. It was an act of stealth
And troubled pleasure. Not without the voice
Of mountain echoes did my boat move on,
Leaving behind her still on either side
Small circles glittering idly in the moon,
Until they melted all into one track
Of sparkling light. A rocky steep uprose
Above the cavern of the willow-tree,
And now, as suited one who proudly rowed
With his best skill, I fixed a steady view
Upon the top of that same craggy ridge,
The bound of the horizon—for behind
Was nothing but the stars and the grey sky.
She was an elfin pinnace; twenty times
I dipped my oars into the silent lake,
And as I rose upon the stroke my boat
Went heaving through the water like a swan—
When from behind that rocky steep, till then
The bound of the horizon, a huge cliff,
As if with voluntary power instinct,
Upreared its head. I struck, and struck again,
And, growing still in stature, the huge cliff

Rose up between me and the stars, and still,
With measured motion, like a living thing
Strode after me. With trembling hands I turned,
And through the silent water stole my way
Back to the cavern of the willow-tree.
There in her mooring-place I left my bark,
And through the meadows homeward went with grave
And serious thoughts; and after I had seen
That spectacle, for many days my brain
Worked with a dim and undetermined sense
Of unknown modes of being. In my thoughts
There was a darkness—call it solitude,
Or blank desertion—no familiar shapes
Of hourly objects, images of trees,
Of sea or sky, no colours of green fields,
But huge and mighty forms that do not live
Like living men moved slowly through my mind
By day, and were the trouble of my dreams.
     Ah, not in vain ye beings of the hills,
And ye that walk the woods and open heaths
By moon or star-light, thus, from my first dawn
Of childhood, did ye love to intertwine
The passions that build up our human soul
Not with the mean and vulgar works of man,
But with high objects, with eternal things,
With life and Nature, purifying thus
The elements of feeling and of thought,
And sanctifying by such discipline
Both pain and fear, until we recognise
A grandeur in the beatings of the heart.
Nor was this fellowship vouchsafed to me
With stinted kindness. In November days,
When vapours rolling down the valleys made
A lonely scene more lonesome, among woods

At noon, and mid the calm of summer nights
When by the margin of the trembling lake
Beneath the gloomy hills I homeward went
In solitude, such intercourse was mine.
    And in the frosty season, when the sun
Was set, and visible for many a mile
The cottage windows through the twilight blazed,
I heeded not the summons. Clear and loud
The village clock tolled six; I wheeled about
Proud and exulting, like an untired horse
That cares not for its home. All shod with steel
We hissed along the polished ice in games
Confederate, imitative of the chace
And woodland pleasures, the resounding horn,
The pack loud bellowing, and the hunted hare.
So through the darkness and the cold we flew,
And not a voice was idle. With the din,
Meanwhile, the precipices rang aloud;
The leafless trees and every icy crag
Tinkled like iron; while the distant hills
Into the tumult sent an alien sound
Of melancholy, not unnoticed; while the stars,
Eastward, were sparkling clear, and in the west
The orange sky of evening died away.
    Not seldom from the uproar I retired
Into a silent bay, or sportively
Glanced sideway, leaving the tumultuous throng,
To cut across the shadow of a star
That gleamed upon the ice. And oftentimes
When we had given our bodies to the wind,
And all the shadowy banks on either side
Came sweeping through the darkness, spinning still
The rapid line of motion, then at once
Have I, reclining back upon my heels,

Stopped short—yet still the solitary cliffs
Wheeled by me, even as if the earth had rolled
With visible motion her diurnal round.
Behind me did they stretch in solemn train,
Feebler and feebler, and I stood and watched
Till all was tranquil as a summer sea.

      Ye powers of earth, ye genii of the springs,
And ye that have your voices in the clouds,
And ye that are familiars of the lakes
And of the standing pools, I may not think
A vulgar hope was yours when ye employed
Such ministry—when ye through many a year
Thus by the agency of boyish sports,
On caves and trees, upon the woods and hills,
Impressed upon all forms the characters
Of danger or desire, and thus did make
The surface of the universal earth
With meanings of delight, of hope and fear,
Work like a sea.

            Not uselessly employed,
I might pursue this theme through every change
Of exercise and sport to which the year
Did summon us in its delightful round.
We were a noisy crew; the sun in heaven
Beheld not vales more beautiful than ours,
Nor saw a race in happiness and joy
More worthy of the fields where they were sown.
I would record with no reluctant voice
Our home amusements by the warm peat fire
At evening, when with pencil and with slate,
In square divisions parcelled out, and all
With crosses and with cyphers scribbled o'er,
We schemed and puzzled, head opposed to head,
In strife too humble to be named in verse;

Or round the naked table, snow-white deal,
Cherry, or maple, sate in close array,
And to the combat—lu or whist—led on
A thick-ribbed army, not as in the world
Discarded and ungratefully thrown by
Even for the very service they had wrought,
But husbanded through many a long campaign.
Oh, with what echoes on the board they fell—
Ironic diamonds, hearts of sable hue,
Queens gleaming through their splendour's last decay,
Knaves wrapt in one assimilating gloom,
And kings indignant at the shame incurred
By royal visages. Meanwhile abroad
The heavy rain was falling, or the frost
Raged bitterly with keen and silent tooth,
And, interrupting the impassioned game,
Oft from the neighbouring lake the splitting ice,
While it sank down towards the water, sent
Among the meadows and the hills its long
And frequent yellings, imitative some
Of wolves that howl along the Bothnic main.

      Nor with less willing heart would I rehearse
The woods of autumn, and their hidden bowers
With milk-white clusters hung; the rod and line—
True symbol of the foolishness of hope—
Which with its strong enchantment led me on
By rocks and pools, where never summer star
Impressed its shadow, to forlorn cascades
Among the windings of the mountain-brooks;
The kite in sultry calms from some high hill
Sent up, ascending thence till it was lost
Among the fleecy clouds—in gusty days
Launched from the lower grounds, and suddenly
Dashed headlong and rejected by the storm.

All these, and more, with rival claims demand
Grateful acknowledgement. It were a song
Venial, and such as—if I rightly judge—
I might protract unblamed, but I perceive
That much is overlooked, and we should ill
Attain our object if, from delicate fears
Of breaking in upon the unity
Of this my argument, I should omit
To speak of such effects as cannot here
Be regularly classed, yet tend no less
To the same point, the growth of mental power
And love of Nature's works.

                    Ere I had seen
Eight summers—and 'twas in the very week
When I was first transplanted to thy vale,
Beloved Hawkshead; when thy paths, thy shores
And brooks, were like a dream of novelty
To my half-infant mind—I chanced to cross
One of those open fields which, shaped like ears,
Make green peninsulas on Esthwaite's lake.
Twilight was coming on, yet through the gloom
I saw distinctly on the opposite shore,
Beneath a tree and close by the lake side,
A heap of garments, as if left by one
Who there was bathing. Half an hour I watched
And no one owned them; meanwhile the calm lake
Grew dark with all the shadows on its breast,
And now and then a leaping fish disturbed
The breathless stillness. The succeeding day
There came a company, and in their boat
Sounded with iron hooks and with long poles.
At length the dead man, mid that beauteous scene
Of trees and hills and water, bolt upright
Rose with his ghastly face. I might advert

To numerous accidents in flood or field,
Quarry or moor, or mid the winter snows,
Distresses and disasters, tragic facts
Of rural history that impressed my mind
With images to which in following years
Far other feelings were attached—with forms
That yet exist with independent life,
And, like their archetypes, know no decay.

      There are in our existence spots of time
Which with distinct preeminence retain
A fructifying virtue, whence, depressed
By trivial occupations and the round
Of ordinary intercourse, our minds—
Especially the imaginative power—
Are nourished and invisibly repaired.
Such moments chiefly seem to have their date
In our first childhood. I remember well
('Tis of an early season that I speak,
The twilight of rememberable life),
While I was yet an urchin, one who scarce
Could hold a bridle, with ambitious hopes
I mounted, and we rode towards the hills.
We were a pair of horsemen: honest James
Was with me, my encourager and guide.
We had not travelled long ere some mischance
Disjoined me from my comrade, and, through fear
Dismounting, down the rough and stony moor
I led my horse, and stumbling on, at length
Came to a bottom where in former times
A man, the murderer of his wife, was hung
In irons. Mouldered was the gibbet-mast;
The bones were gone, the iron and the wood;
Only a long green ridge of turf remained
Whose shape was like a grave. I left the spot,

And reascending the bare slope I saw
A naked pool that lay beneath the hills,
The beacon on the summit, and more near
A girl who bore a pitcher on her head
And seemed with difficult steps to force her way
Against the blowing wind. It was in truth
An ordinary sight, but I should need
Colours and words that are unknown to man
To paint the visionary dreariness
Which, while I looked all round for my lost guide,
Did at that time invest the naked pool,
The beacon on the lonely eminence,
The woman and her garments vexed and tossed
By the strong wind.

            Nor less I recollect—
Long after, though my childhood had not ceased—
Another scene which left a kindred power
Implanted in my mind. One Christmas time,
The day before the holidays began,
Feverish, and tired, and restless, I went forth
Into the fields, impatient for the sight
Of those three horses which should bear us home,
My brothers and myself. There was a crag,
An eminence, which from the meeting-point
Of two highways ascending overlooked
At least a long half-mile of those two roads,
By each of which the expected steeds might come—
The choice uncertain. Thither I repaired
Up to the highest summit. 'Twas a day
Stormy, and rough, and wild, and on the grass
I sate half sheltered by a naked wall.
Upon my right hand was a single sheep,
A whistling hawthorn on my left, and there,
Those two companions at my side, I watched

With eyes intensely straining, as the mist
Gave intermitting prospects of the wood
And plain beneath. Ere I to school returned
That dreary time, ere I had been ten days
A dweller in my father's house, he died,
And I and my two brothers, orphans then,
Followed his body to the grave. The event,
With all the sorrow which it brought, appeared
A chastisement; and when I called to mind
That day so lately passed, when from the crag
I looked in such anxiety of hope,
With trite reflections of morality,
Yet with the deepest passion, I bowed low
To God who thus corrected my desires.
And afterwards the wind and sleety rain,
And all the business of the elements,
The single sheep, and the one blasted tree,
And the bleak music of that old stone wall,
The noise of wood and water, and the mist
Which on the line of each of those two roads
Advanced in such indisputable shapes—
All these were spectacles and sounds to which
I often would repair, and thence would drink
As at a fountain. And I do not doubt
That in this later time, when storm and rain
Beat on my roof at midnight, or by day
When I am in the woods, unknown to me
The workings of my spirit thence are brought.
    Nor, sedulous as I have been to trace
How Nature by collateral interest,
And by extrinsic passion, peopled first
My mind with forms or beautiful or grand
And made me love them, may I well forget
How other pleasures have been mine, and joys

Of subtler origin—how I have felt
Not seldom, even in that tempestuous time,
Those hallowed and pure motions of the sense
Which seem in their simplicity to own
An intellectual charm, that calm delight
Which, if I err not, surely must belong
To those first-born affinities that fit
Our new existence to existing things,
And, in our dawn of being, constitute
The bond of union betwixt life and joy.

      Yes, I remember when the changeful earth
And twice five seasons on my mind had stamped
The faces of the moving year, even then,
A child, I held unconscious intercourse
With the eternal beauty, drinking in
A pure organic pleasure from the lines
Of curling mist, or from the level plain
Of waters coloured by the steady clouds.
The sands of Westmoreland, the creeks and bays
Of Cumbria's rocky limits, they can tell
How when the sea threw off his evening shade
And to the shepherd's hut beneath the crags
Did send sweet notice of the rising moon,
How I have stood, to images like these
A stranger, linking with the spectacle
No body of associated forms,
And bringing with me no peculiar sense
Of quietness or peace—yet I have stood
Even while my eye has moved o'er three long leagues
Of shining water, gathering, as it seemed,
Through the wide surface of that field of light
New pleasure, like a bee among the flowers.

      Thus often in those fits of vulgar joy
Which through all seasons on a child's pursuits

Are prompt attendants, mid that giddy bliss
Which like a tempest works along the blood
And is forgotten, even then I felt
Gleams like the flashing of a shield. The earth
And common face of Nature spake to me
Rememberable things—sometimes, 'tis true,
By quaint associations, yet not vain
Nor profitless, if haply they impressed
Collateral objects and appearances,
Albeit lifeless then, and doomed to sleep
Until maturer seasons called them forth
To impregnate and to elevate the mind.
And if the vulgar joy by its own weight
Wearied itself out of the memory,
The scenes which were a witness of that joy
Remained, in their substantial lineaments
Depicted on the brain, and to the eye
Were visible, a daily sight. And thus
By the impressive agency of fear,
By pleasure and repeated happiness—
So frequently repeated—and by force
Of obscure feelings representative
Of joys that were forgotten, these same scenes,
So beauteous and majestic in themselves,
Though yet the day was distant, did at length
Become habitually dear, and all
Their hues and forms were by invisible links
Allied to the affections.

I began
My story early, feeling, as I fear,
The weakness of a human love for days
Disowned by memory—ere the birth of spring
Planting my snowdrops among winter snows.
Nor will it seem to thee, my friend, so prompt

In sympathy, that I have lengthened out
With fond and feeble tongue a tedious tale.
Meanwhile my hope has been that I might fetch
Reproaches from my former years, whose power
May spur me on, in manhood now mature,
To honourable toil. Yet should it be
That this is but an impotent desire—
That I by such inquiry am not taught
To understand myself, nor thou to know
With better knowledge how the heart was framed
Of him thou lovest—need I dread from thee
Harsh judgements if I am so loth to quit
Those recollected hours that have the charm
Of visionary things, and lovely forms
And sweet sensations, that throw back our life
And make our infancy a visible scene
On which the sun is shining?

SECOND PART

Thus far, my friend, have we retraced the way
Through which I travelled when I first began
To love the woods and fields. The passion yet
Was in its birth, sustained, as might befal,
By nourishment that came unsought—for still
From week to week, from month to month, we lived
A round of tumult. Duly were our games
Prolonged in summer till the daylight failed:
No chair remained before the doors, the bench
And threshold steps were empty, fast asleep
The labourer and the old man who had sate
A later lingerer, yet the revelry
Continued and the loud uproar. At last,
When all the ground was dark and the huge clouds

Were edged with twinkling stars, to bed we went
With weary joints and with a beating mind.
Ah, is there one who ever has been young
And needs a monitory voice to tame
The pride of virtue and of intellect?
And is there one, the wisest and the best
Of all mankind, who does not sometimes wish
For things which cannot be, who would not give,
If so he might, to duty and to truth
The eagerness of infantine desire?
A tranquillizing spirit presses now
On my corporeal frame, so wide appears
The vacancy between me and those days,
Which yet have such self-presence in my heart
That sometimes when I think of them I seem
Two consciousnesses—conscious of myself,
And of some other being.

                    A grey stone
Of native rock, left midway in the square
Of our small market-village, was the home
And centre of these joys; and when, returned
After long absence thither I repaired,
I found that it was split and gone to build
A smart assembly-room that perked and flared
With wash and rough-cast, elbowing the ground
Which had been ours. But let the fiddle scream,
And be ye happy! Yet I know, my friends,
That more than one of you will think with me
Of those soft starry nights, and that old dame
From whom the stone was named, who there had sate
And watched her table with its huckster's wares,
Assiduous, for the length of sixty years.

      We ran a boisterous race, the year span round
With giddy motion; but the time approached

That brought with it a regular desire
For calmer pleasures—when the beauteous scenes
Of Nature were collaterally attached
To every scheme of holiday delight,
And every boyish sport, less grateful else
And languidly pursued. When summer came
It was the pastime of our afternoons
To beat along the plain of Windermere
With rival oars; and the selected bourn
Was now an island musical with birds
That sang for ever, now a sister isle
Beneath the oak's umbrageous covert, sown
With lilies-of-the-valley like a field,
And now a third small island where remained
An old stone table and one mouldered cave—
A hermit's history. In such a race,
So ended, disappointment could be none,
Uneasiness, or pain, or jealousy;
We rested in the shade, all pleased alike,
Conquered or conqueror. Thus our selfishness
Was mellowed down, and thus the pride of strength
And the vainglory of superior skill
Were interfused with objects which subdued
And tempered them, and gradually produced
A quiet independence of the heart.
And to my friend who knows me I may add,
Unapprehensive of reproof, that hence
Ensued a diffidence and modesty,
And I was taught to feel—perhaps too much—
The self-sufficing power of solitude.
　　　No delicate viands sapped our bodily strength:
More than we wished we knew the blessing then
Of vigorous hunger, for our daily meals
Were frugal, Sabine fare—and then, exclude

A little weekly stipend, and we lived
Through three divisions of the quartered year
In pennyless poverty. But now, to school
Returned from the half-yearly holidays,
We came with purses more profusely filled,
Allowance which abundantly sufficed
To gratify the palate with repasts
More costly than the dame of whom I spake,
That ancient woman, and her board, supplied.
Hence inroads into distant vales, and long
Excursions far away among the hills,
Hence rustic dinners on the cool green ground—
Or in the woods, or by a river-side
Or fountain—festive banquets, that provoked
The languid action of a natural scene
By pleasure of corporeal appetite.
    Nor is my aim neglected if I tell
How twice in the long length of those half-years
We from our funds perhaps with bolder hand
Drew largely, anxious for one day at least
To feel the motion of the galloping steed;
And with the good old inkeeper, in truth
I needs must say, that sometimes we have used
Sly subterfuge, for the intended bound
Of the day's journey was too distant far
For any cautious man: a structure famed
Beyond its neighbourhood, the antique walls
Of a large abbey, with its fractured arch,
Belfry, and images, and living trees—
A holy scene. Along the smooth green turf
Our horses grazed. In more than inland peace,
Left by the winds that overpass the vale,
In that sequestered ruin trees and towers—
Both silent and both motionless alike—

Hear all day long the murmuring sea that beats
Incessantly upon a craggy shore.
      Our steeds remounted, and the summons given,
With whip and spur we by the chantry flew
In uncouth race, and left the cross-legged knight
And the stone abbot, and that single wren
Which one day sang so sweetly in the nave
Of the old church that, though from recent showers
The earth was comfortless, and, touched by faint
Internal breezes, from the roofless walls
The shuddering ivy dripped large drops, yet still
So sweetly mid the gloom the invisible bird
Sang to itself that there I could have made
My dwelling-place, and lived for ever there,
To hear such music. Through the walls we flew
And down the valley, and, a circuit made
In wantonness of heart, through rough and smooth
We scampered homeward. O, ye rocks and streams,
And that still spirit of the evening air,
Even in this joyous time I sometimes felt
Your presence, when, with slackened step, we breathed
Along the sides of the steep hills, or when,
Lightened by gleams of moonlight from the sea,
We beat with thundering hoofs the level sand.
      There was a row of ancient trees, since fallen,
That on the margin of a jutting land
Stood near the lake of Coniston, and made,
With its long boughs above the water stretched,
A gloom through which a boat might sail along
As in a cloister. An old hall was near,
Grotesque and beautiful, its gavel-end
And huge round chimneys to the top o'ergrown
With fields of ivy. Thither we repaired—
'Twas even a custom with us—to the shore,

And to that cool piazza. They who dwelt
In the neglected mansion-house supplied
Fresh butter, tea-kettle and earthernware,
And chafing-dish with smoking coals; and so
Beneath the trees we sate in our small boat,
And in the covert eat our delicate meal
Upon the calm smooth lake. It was a joy
Worthy the heart of one who is full grown
To rest beneath those horizontal boughs
And mark the radiance of the setting sun,
Himself unseen, reposing on the top
Of the high eastern hills. And there I said,
That beauteous sight before me, there I said
(Then first beginning in my thoughts to mark
That sense of dim similitude which links
Our moral feelings with external forms)
That in whatever region I should close
My mortal life I would remember you,
Fair scenes—that dying I would think on you,
My soul would send a longing look to you,
Even as that setting sun, while all the vale
Could nowhere catch one faint memorial gleam,
Yet with the last remains of his last light
Still lingered, and a farewell lustre threw
On the dear mountain-tops where first he rose.
'Twas then my fourteenth summer, and these words
Were uttered in a casual access
Of sentiment, a momentary trance
That far outran the habit of my mind.

      Upon the eastern shore of Windermere
Above the crescent of a pleasant bay
There was an inn, no homely-featured shed,
Brother of the surrounding cottages,
But 'twas a splendid place, the door beset

With chaises, grooms, and liveries, and within
Decanters, glasses and the blood-red wine.
In ancient times, or ere the hall was built
On the large island, had the dwelling been
More worthy of a poet's love, a hut
Proud of its one bright fire and sycamore shade;
But though the rhymes were gone which once inscribed
The threshold, and large golden characters
On the blue-frosted signboard had usurped
The place of the old lion, in contempt
And mockery of the rustic painter's hand,
Yet to this hour the spot to me is dear
With all its foolish pomp. The garden lay
Upon a slope surmounted by the plain
Of a small bowling-green; beneath us stood
A grove, with gleams of water through the trees
And over the tree-tops—nor did we want
Refreshment, strawberries and mellow cream—
And there through half an afternoon we played
On the smooth platform, and the shouts we sent
Made all the mountains ring. But ere the fall
Of night, when in our pinnace we returned
Over the dusky lake, and to the beach
Of some small island steered our course, with one,
The minstrel of our troop, and left him there,
And rowed off gently, while he blew his flute
Alone upon the rock, oh, then the calm
And dead still water lay upon my mind
Even with a weight of pleasure, and the sky,
Never before so beautiful, sank down
Into my heart and held me like a dream.
　　Thus day by day my sympathies increased,
And thus the common range of visible things
Grew dear to me. Already I began

To love the sun—a boy I loved the sun
Not as I since have loved him (as a pledge
And surety of my earthly life, a light
Which while I view I feel I am alive),
But for this cause, that I had seen him lay
His beauty on the morning hills, had seen
The western mountain touch his setting orb
In many a thoughtless hour, when from excess
Of happiness my blood appeared to flow
With its own pleasure, and I breathed with joy.
And from like feelings, humble though intense,
To patriotic and domestic love
Analogous, the moon to me was dear:
For I would dream away my purposes
Standing to look upon her, while she hung
Midway between the hills as if she knew
No other region but belonged to thee,
Yea appertained by a peculiar right
To thee and thy grey huts, my native vale.

      Those incidental charms which first attached
My heart to rural objects, day by day
Grew weaker, and I hasten on to tell
How Nature, intervenient till this time
And secondary, now at length was sought
For her own sake. But who shall parcel out
His intellect by geometric rules
Split like a province into round and square?
Who knows the individual hour in which
His habits were first sown even as a seed?
Who that shall point as with a wand, and say
'This portion of the river of my mind
Came from yon fountain'? Thou, my friend, art one
More deeply read in thy own thoughts, no slave
Of that false secondary power by which

In weakness we create distinctions, then
Believe our puny boundaries are things
Which we perceive, and not which we have made.
To thee, unblinded by these outward shews,
The unity of all has been revealed;
And thou wilt doubt with me, less aptly skilled
Than many are to class the cabinet
Of their sensations, and in voluble phrase
Run through the history and birth of each
As of a single independent thing.
Hard task to analyse a soul, in which
Not only general habits and desires,
But each most obvious and particular thought—
Not in a mystical and idle sense,
But in the words of reason deeply weighed—
Hath no beginning.
                            Blessed the infant babe—
For with my best conjectures I would trace
The progress of our being—blest the babe
Nursed in his mother's arms, the babe who sleeps
Upon his mother's breast, who, when his soul
Claims manifest kindred with an earthly soul,
Doth gather passion from his mother's eye.
Such feelings pass into his torpid life
Like an awakening breeze, and hence his mind,
Even in the first trial of its powers,
Is prompt and watchful, eager to combine
In one appearance all the elements
And parts of the same object, else detached
And loth to coalesce. Thus day by day,
Subjected to the discipline of love,
His organs and recipient faculties
Are quickened, are more vigorous; his mind spreads,
Tenacious of the forms which it receives.

In one beloved presence—nay and more,
In that most apprehensive habitude
And those sensations which have been derived
From this beloved presence—there exists
A virtue which irradiates and exalts
All objects through all intercourse of sense.
No outcast he, bewildered and depressed;
Along his infant veins are interfused
The gravitation and the filial bond
Of Nature that connect him with the world.
Emphatically such a being lives,
An inmate of this *active* universe.
From Nature largely he receives, nor so
Is satisfied, but largely gives again;
For feeling has to him imparted strength,
And—powerful in all sentiments of grief,
Of exultation, fear and joy—his mind,
Even as an agent of the one great mind,
Creates, creator and receiver both,
Working but in alliance with the works
Which it beholds. Such, verily, is the first
Poetic spirit of our human life—
By uniform control of after years
In most abated and suppressed, in some
Through every change of growth or of decay
Preeminent till death.

               From early days,
Beginning not long after that first time
In which, a babe, by intercourse of touch
I held mute dialogues with my mother's heart,
I have endeavoured to display the means
Whereby this infant sensibility,
Great birthright of our being, was in me
Augmented and sustained. Yet is a path

More difficult before me, and I fear
That in its broken windings we shall need
The chamois' sinews and the eagle's wing.
For now a trouble came into my mind
From obscure causes. I was left alone
Seeking this visible world, nor knowing why.
The props of my affections were removed,
And yet the building stood, as if sustained
By its own spirit. All that I beheld
Was dear to me, and from this cause it came
That now to Nature's finer influxes
My mind lay open—to that more exact
And intimate communion which our hearts
Maintain with the minuter properties
Of objects which already are beloved,
And of those only.
             Many are the joys
Of youth, but oh, what happiness to live
When every hour brings palpable access
Of knowledge, when all knowledge is delight,
And sorrow is not there. The seasons came,
And every season brought a countless store
Of modes and temporary qualities
Which but for this most watchful power of love
Had been neglected, left a register
Of permanent relations else unknown.
Hence life, and change, and beauty, solitude
More active even than 'best society',
Society made sweet as solitude
By silent inobtrusive sympathies,
And gentle agitations of the mind
From manifold distinctions—difference
Perceived in things where to the common eye
No difference is—and hence, from the same source,

Sublimer joy. For I would walk alone
In storm and tempest, or in starlight nights
Beneath the quiet heavens, and at that time
Would feel whate'er there is of power in sound
To breathe an elevated mood, by form
Or image unprofaned; and I would stand
Beneath some rock, listening to sounds that are
The ghostly language of the ancient earth,
Or make their dim abode in distant winds.
Thence did I drink the visionary power.
I deem not profitless these fleeting moods
Of shadowy exaltation; not for this,
That they are kindred to our purer mind
And intellectual life, but that the soul—
Remembering how she felt, but what she felt
Remembering not—retains an obscure sense
Of possible sublimity, to which
With growing faculties she doth aspire,
With faculties still growing, feeling still
That whatsoever point they gain they still
Have something to pursue.
                              And not alone
In grandeur and in tumult, but no less
In tranquil scenes, that universal power
And fitness in the latent qualities
And essences of things, by which the mind
Is moved with feelings of delight, to me
Came strengthened with a superadded soul,
A virtue not its own. My morning walks
Were early: oft before the hours of school
I travelled round our little lake, five miles
Of pleasant wandering—happy time, more dear
For this, that one was by my side, a friend
Then passionately loved. With heart how full

Will he peruse these lines, this page—perhaps
A blank to other men—for many years
Have since flowed in between us, and, our minds
Both silent to each other, at this time
We live as if those hours had never been
Nor seldom did I lift our cottage latch
Far earlier, and before the vernal thrush
Was audible, among the hills I sate
Alone upon some jutting eminence
At the first hour of morning, when the vale
Lay quiet in an utter solitude.
How shall I trace the history, where seek
The origin of what I then have felt?
Oft in those moments such a holy calm
Did overspread my soul that I forgot
The agency of sight, and what I saw
Appeared like something in myself, a dream,
A prospect in my mind.
                  'Twere long to tell
What spring and autumn, what the winter snows,
And what the summer shade, what day and night,
The evening and the morning, what my dreams
And what my waking thoughts, supplied to nurse
That spirit of religious love in which
I walked with Nature. But let this at least
Be not forgotten, that I still retained
My first creative sensibility,
That by the regular action of the world
My soul was unsubdued. A plastic power
Abode with me, a forming hand, at times
Rebellious, acting in a devious mood,
A local spirit of its own, at war
With general tendency, but for the most
Subservient strictly to the external things

With which it communed. An auxiliar light
Came from my mind, which on the setting sun
Bestowed new splendour; the melodious birds,
The gentle breezes, fountains that ran on
Murmuring so sweetly in themselves, obeyed
A like dominion, and the midnight storm
Grew darker in the presence of my eye.
Hence my obeisance, my devotion hence,
And *hence* my transport.

                Nor should this, perchance,
Pass unrecorded, that I still had loved
The exercise and produce of a toil
Than analytic industry to me
More pleasing, and whose character I deem
Is more poetic, as resembling more
Creative agency—I mean to speak
Of that interminable building reared
By observation of affinities
In objects where no brotherhood exists
To common minds. My seventeenth year was come,
And, whether from this habit rooted now
So deeply in my mind, or from excess
Of the great social principle of life
Coercing all things into sympathy,
To unorganic natures I transferred
My own enjoyments, or, the power of truth
Coming in revelation, I conversed
With things that really are, I at this time
Saw blessings spread around me like a sea.
Thus did my days pass on, and now at length
From Nature and her overflowing soul
I had received so much that all my thoughts
Were steeped in feeling. I was only then
Contented when with bliss ineffable

I felt the sentiment of being spread
O'er all that moves, and all that seemeth still,
O'er all that, lost beyond the reach of thought
And human knowledge, to the human eye
Invisible, yet liveth to the heart,
O'er all that leaps, and runs, and shouts, and sings,
Or beats the gladsome air, o'er all that glides
Beneath the wave, yea, in the wave itself
And mighty depth of waters. Wonder not
If such my transports were, for in all things
I saw one life, and felt that it was joy;
One song they sang and it was audible—
Most audible then when the fleshly ear,
O'ercome by grosser prelude of that strain,
Forgot its functions and slept undisturbed.

  If this be error, and another faith
Find easier access to the pious mind,
Yet were I grossly destitute of all
Those human sentiments which make this earth
So dear if I should fail with grateful voice
To speak of you, ye mountains, and ye lakes
And sounding cataracts, ye mists and winds
That dwell among the hills where I was born.
If in my youth I have been pure in heart,
If, mingling with the world, I am content
With my own modest pleasures, and have lived
With God and Nature communing, removed
From little enmities and low desires,
The gift is yours; if in these times of fear,
This melancholy waste of hopes o'erthrown,
If, mid indifference and apathy
And wicked exultation, when good men
On every side fall off we know not how
To selfishness, disguised in gentle names

Of peace and quiet and domestic love—
Yet mingled, not unwillingly, with sneers
On visionary minds—if, in this time
Of dereliction and dismay, I yet
Despair not of our nature, but retain
A more than Roman confidence, a faith
That fails not, in all sorrow my support,
The blessing of my life, the gift is yours
Ye mountains, thine O Nature. Thou hast fed
My lofty speculations, and in thee
For this uneasy heart of ours I find
A never-failing principle of joy
And purest passion.

                Thou, my friend, wast reared
In the great city, mid far other scenes,
But we by different roads at length have gained
The self-same bourne. And from this cause to thee
I speak unapprehensive of contempt,
The insinuated scoff of coward tongues,
And all that silent language which so oft
In conversation betwixt man and man
Blots from the human countenance all trace
Of beauty and of love. For thou hast sought
The truth in solitude, and thou art one
The most intense of Nature's worshippers,
In many things my brother, chiefly here
In this my deep devotion. Fare thee well:
Health and the quiet of a healthful mind
Attend thee, seeking oft the haunts of men—
But yet more often living with thyself,
And for thyself—so haply shall thy days
Be many, and a blessing to mankind.

from *The Prelude (1805)*

BOOK FOURTH

SUMMER VACATION

. . . .

A favourite pleasure hath it been with me,
From time of earliest youth, to walk alone
Along the public Way, when, for the night
Deserted, in its silence it assumes
A character of deeper quietness
Than pathless solitudes. At such an hour
Once, ere these summer months were pass'd away,
I slowly mounted up a steep ascent
Where the road's watery surface, to the ridge
Of that sharp rising, glitter'd in the moon,
And seem'd before my eyes another stream
Creeping with silent lapse to join the brook
That murmur'd in the valley. On I went
Tranquil, receiving in my own despite
Amusement, as I slowly pass'd along,
From such near objects as from time to time
Perforce intruded on the listless sense
Quiescent, and dispos'd to sympathy,
With an exhausted mind, worn out by toil,
And all unworthy of the deeper joy
Which waits on distant prospect, cliff, or sea,
The dark blue vault, and universe of stars.
Thus did I steal along that silent road,
My body from the stillness drinking in
A restoration like the calm of sleep,
But sweeter far. Above, before, behind,

Around me, all was peace and solitude,
I look'd not round, nor did the solitude
Speak to my eye; but it was heard and felt.
O happy state! what beauteous pictures now
Rose in harmonious imagery—they rose
As from some distant region of my soul
And came along like dreams; yet such as left
Obscurely mingled with their passing forms
A consciousness of animal delight,
A self-possession felt in every pause
And every gentle movement of my frame.
   While thus I wander'd, step by step led on,
It chanc'd a sudden turning of the road
Presented to my view an uncouth shape
So near, that, slipping back into the shade
Of a thick hawthorn, I could mark him well,
Myself unseen. He was of stature tall,
A foot above man's common measure tall,
Stiff in his form, and upright, lank and lean;
A man more meagre, as it seem'd to me,
Was never seen abroad by night or day.
His arms were long, and bare his hands; his mouth
Shew'd ghastly in the moonlight: from behind
A milestone propp'd him, and his figure seem'd
Half-sitting, and half-standing. I could mark
That he was clad in military garb,
Though faded, yet entire. He was alone,
Had no attendant, neither Dog, nor Staff,
Nor knapsack; in his very dress appear'd
A desolation, a simplicity
That seem'd akin to solitude. Long time
Did I peruse him with a mingled sense
Of fear and sorrow. From his lips, meanwhile,
There issued murmuring sounds, as if of pain

Or of uneasy thought; yet still his form
Kept the same steadiness; and at his feet
His shadow lay, and mov'd not. In a Glen
Hard by, a Village stood, whose roofs and doors
Were visible among the scatter'd trees,
Scarce distant from the spot an arrow's flight;
I wish'd to see him move; but he remain'd
Fix'd to his place, and still from time to time
Sent forth a murmuring voice of dead complaint,
Groans scarcely audible. Without self-blame
I had not thus prolong'd my watch, and now,
Subduing my heart's specious cowardice
I left the shady nook where I had stood,
And hail'd him. Slowly from his resting-place
He rose, and with a lean and wasted arm
In measur'd gesture lifted to his head,
Return'd my salutation; then resum'd
His station as before: and when, erelong,
I ask'd his history, he in reply
Was neither slow nor eager; but unmov'd,
And with a quiet, uncomplaining voice,
A stately air of mild indifference,
He told, in simple words, a Soldier's tale,
That in the Tropic Islands he had serv'd,
Whence he had landed, scarcely ten days past,
That on his landing he had been dismiss'd,
And now was travelling to his native home.
At this, I turn'd and looked towards the Village
But all were gone to rest; the fires all out;
And every silent window to the Moon
Shone with a yellow glitter. 'No one there,'
Said I, 'is waking, we must measure back
The way which we have come: behind yon wood
A Labourer dwells; and, take it on my word

He will not murmur should we break his rest;
And with a ready heart will give you food
And lodging for the night.' At this he stoop'd,
And from the ground took up an oaken Staff,
By me yet unobserv'd, a traveller's Staff;
Which, I suppose, from his slack hand had dropp'd,
And lain till now neglected in the grass.

   Towards the Cottage without more delay
We shap'd our course; as it appear'd to me,
He travell'd without pain, and I beheld
With ill-suppress'd astonishment his tall
And ghastly figure moving at my side;
Nor, while we journey'd thus could I forbear
To question him of what he had endur'd
From hardship, battle, or the pestilence.
He, all the while, was in demeanour calm,
Concise in answer; solemn and sublime
He might have seem'd, but that in all he said
There was a strange half-absence, and a tone
Of weakness and indifference, as of one
Remembering the importance of his theme
But feeling it no longer. We advanced
Slowly, and, ere we to the wood were come
Discourse had ceas'd. Together on we pass'd,
In silence, through the shades, gloomy and dark;
Then, turning up along an open field
We gain'd the Cottage. At the door I knock'd,
Calling aloud 'my Friend, here is a Man
By sickness overcome; beneath your roof
This night let him find rest, and give him food,
If food he need, for he is faint and tired.'
Assur'd that now my Comrade would repose
In comfort, I entreated that henceforth

He would not linger in the public ways
But ask for timely furtherance and help
Such as his state requir'd. At this reproof,
With the same ghastly mildness in his look
He said 'my trust is in the God of Heaven
And in the eye of him that passes me.'
The Cottage door was speedily unlock'd,
And now the Soldier touch'd his hat again
With his lean hand; and in a voice that seem'd
To speak with a reviving interest,
Till then unfelt, he thank'd me; I return'd
The blessing of the poor unhappy Man;
And so we parted. Back I cast a look,
And linger'd near the door a little space;
Then sought with quiet heart my distant home.

BOOK SIXTH

CAMBRIDGE AND THE ALPS

. . . .
A passing word erewhile did lightly touch
On wanderings of my own; and now to these
My Poem leads me with an easier mind.
The employments of three winters when I wore
A student's gown have been already told,
Or shadow'd forth, as far as there is need.
When the third summer brought its liberty
A Fellow Student and myself, he, too,
A Mountaineer, together sallied forth
And, Staff in hand, on foot pursu'd our way
Towards the distant Alps. An open slight
Of College cares and study was the scheme,
Nor entertain'd without concern for those

To whom my worldly interests were dear:
But Nature then was sovereign in my heart,
And mighty forms seizing a youthful Fancy
Had given a charter to irregular hopes.
In any age, without an impulse sent
From work of Nations, and their goings-on,
I should have been possessed by like desire:
But 'twas a time when Europe was rejoiced,
France standing on the top of golden hours,
And human nature seeming born again.
Bound, as I said, to the Alps, it was our lot
To land at Calais on the very eve
Of that great federal Day; and there we saw,
In a mean City, and among a few,
How bright a face is worn when joy of one
Is joy of tens of millions. Southward thence
We took our way direct through Hamlets, Towns,
Gaudy with reliques of that Festival,
Flowers left to wither on triumphal Arcs,
And window-Garlands. On the public roads,
And, once, three days successively, through paths
By which our toilsome journey was abridg'd,
Among sequester'd villages we walked,
And found benevolence and blessedness
Spread like a fragrance everywhere, like Spring
That leaves no corner of the land untouch'd.
Where Elms, for many and many a league, in files,
With their thin umbrage, on the stately roads
Of that great Kingdom, rustled o'er our heads,
For ever near us as we paced along,
'Twas sweet at such a time, with such delights
On every side, in prime of youthful strength,
To feed a Poet's tender melancholy
And fond conceit of sadness, to the noise

And gentle undulations which they made.
Unhous'd, beneath the Evening Star we saw
Dances of liberty, and, in late hours
Of darkness, dances in the open air.
Among the vine-clad Hills of Burgundy,
Upon the bosom of the gentle Soane
We glided forward with the flowing stream:
Swift Rhone, thou wert the wings on which we cut
Between thy lofty rocks! Enchanting show
Those woods, and farms, and orchards did present,
And single Cottages, and lurking Towns,
Reach after reach, procession without end
Of deep and stately Vales. A lonely Pair
Of Englishmen we were, and sail'd along
Cluster'd together with a merry crowd
Of those emancipated, with a host
Of Travellers, chiefly Delegates, returning
From the great Spousals newly solemniz'd
At their chief City in the sight of Heaven.
Like bees they swarm'd, gaudy and gay as bees;
Some vapour'd in the unruliness of joy
And flourish'd with their swords, as if to fight
The saucy air. In this blithe Company
We landed, took with them our evening Meal,
Guests welcome almost as the Angels were
To Abraham of old. The Supper done,
With flowing cups elate, and happy thoughts,
We rose at signal giv'n, and form'd a ring
And, hand in hand, danced round and round the Board;
All hearts were open, every tongue was loud
With amity and glee; we bore a name
Honour'd in France, the name of Englishmen,
And hospitably did they give us hail
As their forerunners in a glorious course,

And round, and round the board they danced again.
With this same throng our voyage we pursu'd
At early dawn; the Monastery Bells
Made a sweet jingling in our youthful ears;
The rapid River flowing without noise,
And every Spire we saw among the rocks
Spake with a sense of peace, at intervals
Touching the heart amid the boisterous Crew
With which we were environ'd. Having parted
From this glad Rout, the Convent of Chartreuse
Received us two days afterwards, and there
We rested in an awful Solitude;
Thence onward to the Country of the Swiss.

BOOK NINTH

RESIDENCE IN FRANCE

. . . .
    For, born in a poor District, and which yet
Retaineth more of ancient homeliness,
Manners erect, and frank simplicity,
Than any other nook of English Land,
It was my fortune scarcely to have seen
Through the whole tenor of my School-day time
The face of one, who, whether Boy or Man,
Was vested with attention or respect
Through claims of wealth or blood; nor was it least
Of many debts which afterwards I owed
To Cambridge, and an academic life
That something there was holden up to view
Of a Republic, where all stood thus far
Upon equal ground, that they were brothers all
In honour, as in one community,

Scholars and Gentlemen, where, furthermore,
Distinction lay open to all that came,
And wealth and titles were in less esteem
Than talents and successful industry.
Add unto this, subservience from the first
To God and Nature's single sovereignty,
Familiar presences of awful Power
And fellowship with venerable books
To sanction the proud workings of the soul,
And mountain liberty. It could not be
But that one tutor'd thus, who had been form'd
To thought and moral feeling in the way
This story hath described, should look with awe
Upon the faculties of Man, receive
Gladly the highest promises, and hail
As best the government of equal rights
And individual worth. And hence, O Friend!
If at the first great outbreak I rejoiced
Less than might well befit my youth, the cause
In part lay here, that unto me the events
Seemed nothing out of nature's certain course,
A gift that rather was come late than soon.
No wonder, then, if advocates like these
Whom I have mention'd, at this riper day
Were impotent to make my hopes put on
The shape of theirs, my understanding bend
In honour to their honour, zeal which yet
Had slumber'd, now in opposition burst
Forth like a Polar Summer; every word
They utter'd was a dart, by counter-winds
Blown back upon themselves, their reason seem'd
Confusion-stricken by a higher power
Than human understanding, their discourse
Maim'd, spiritless, and in their weakness strong

I triumph'd.
             Meantime, day by day, the roads
(While I consorted with these Royalists)
Were crowded with the bravest Youth of France,
And all the promptest of her Spirits, link'd
In gallant Soldiership, and posting on
To meet the War upon her Frontier Bounds.
Yet at this very moment do tears start
Into mine eyes; I do not say I weep,
I wept not then, but tears have dimm'd my sight,
In memory of the farewells of that time,
Domestic severings, female fortitude
At dearest separation, patriot love
And self-devotion, and terrestrial hope
Encourag'd with a martyr's confidence;
Even files of Strangers merely, seen but once,
And for a moment, men from far with sound
Of music, martial tunes, and banners spread
Entering the City, here and there a face
Or person singled out among the rest,
Yet still a Stranger and belov'd as such,
Even by these passing spectacles my heart
Was oftentimes uplifted, and they seem'd
Like arguments from Heaven, that 'twas a cause
Good, and which no one could stand up against
Who was not lost, abandon'd, selfish, proud,
Mean, miserable, wilfully deprav'd,
Hater perverse of equity and truth.
    Among that band of Officers was one
Already hinted at, of other mold,
A Patriot, thence rejected by the rest
And with an oriental loathing spurn'd,
As of a different Cast. A meeker Man
Than this liv'd never, or a more benign

Meek, though enthusiastic to the height
Of highest expectation. Injuries
Made *him* more gracious, and his nature then
Did breathe its sweetness out most sensibly
As aromatic flowers on alpine turf
When foot hath crush'd them. He thro' the events
Of that great change wander'd in perfect faith,
As through a Book, an old Romance or Tale
Of Fairy, or some dream of actions wrought
Behind the summer clouds. By birth he rank'd
With the most noble, but unto the poor
Among mankind he was in service bound
As by some tie invisible, oaths profess'd
To a religious Order. Man he lov'd
As Man; and to the mean and the obscure
And all the homely in their homely works
Transferr'd a courtesy which had no air
Of condescension, but did rather seem
A passion and a gallantry, like that
Which he, a Soldier, in his idler day
Had pay'd to Woman; somewhat vain he was,
Or seem'd so, yet it was not vanity
But fondness, and a kind of radiant joy
That cover'd him about when he was bent
On works of love or freedom, or revolved
Complacently the progress of a cause,
Whereof he was a part; yet this was meek
And placid, and took nothing from the Man
That was delightful: oft in solitude
With him did I discourse about the end
Of civil government, and its wisest forms,
Of ancient prejudice, and chartered rights,
Allegiance, faith, and law by time matured,
Custom and habit, novelty and change,

Of self-respect, and virtue in the Few
For patrimonial honour set apart,
And ignorance in the labouring Multitude.
For he, an upright Man and tolerant,
Balanced these contemplations in his mind
And I, who at that time was scarcely dipp'd
Into the turmoil, had a sounder judgment
Than afterwards, carried about me yet
With less alloy to its integrity
The experience of past ages, as through help
Of Books and common life it finds its way
To youthful minds, by objects over near
Not press'd upon, nor dazzled or misled
By struggling with the crowd for present ends.
. . . .
                                And when we chanc'd
One day to meet a hunger-bitten Girl,
Who crept along, fitting her languid self
Unto a Heifer's motion, by a cord
Tied to her arm, and picking thus from the lane
Its sustenance, while the Girl with her two hands
Was busy knitting, in a heartless mood
Of solitude, and at the sight my Friend
In agitation said, ' 'Tis against *that*
Which we are fighting,' I with him believed
Devoutly that a spirit was abroad
Which could not be withstood, that poverty
At least like this, would in a little time
Be found no more, that we should see the earth
Unthwarted in her wish to recompense
The industrious, and the lowly Child of Toil,
All institutes for ever blotted out
That legalised exclusion, empty pomp
Abolish'd, sensual state and cruel power

Whether by edict of the one or few,
And finally, as sum and crown of all,
Should see the People having a strong hand
In making their own Laws, whence better days
To all mankind. But, these things set apart,
Was not the single confidence enough
To animate the mind that ever turn'd
A thought to human welfare, that henceforth
Captivity by mandate without law
Should cease, and open accusation lead
To sentence in the hearing of the world
And open punishment, if not the air
Be free to breathe in, and the heart of Man
Dread nothing.

BOOK TENTH

RESIDENCE IN FRANCE

. . . .
And now the strength of Britain was put forth
In league with the confederated Host,
Not in my single self alone I found,
But in the minds of all ingenuous Youth,
Change and subversion from this hour. No shock
Given to my moral nature had I known
Down to that very moment; neither lapse
Nor turn of sentiment that might be nam'd
A revolution, save at this one time,
All else was progress on the self-same path
On which with a diversity of pace
I had been travelling; this a stride at once
Into another region. True it is,
'Twas not conceal'd with what ungracious eyes

Our native Rulers from the very first
Had look'd upon regenerated France
Nor had I doubted that this day would come.
But in such contemplation I had thought
Of general interests only, beyond this
Had [never] once foretasted the event.
Now had I other business for I felt
The ravage of this most unnatural strife
In my own heart; there lay it like a weight
At enmity with all the tenderest springs
Of my enjoyments. I, who with the breeze
Had play'd, a green leaf on the blessed tree
Of my beloved country; nor had wish'd
For happier fortune than to wither there,
Now from my pleasant station was cut off,
And toss'd about in whirlwinds. I rejoic'd,
Yea, afterwards, truth most painful to record!
Exulted in the triumph of my soul
When Englishmen by thousands were o'erthrown,
Left without glory on the Field, or driven,
Brave hearts, to shameful flight. It was a grief,
Grief call it not, 'twas anything but that,
A conflict of sensations without name,
Of which he only who may love the sight
Of a Village Steeple as I do can judge
When in the Congregation, bending all
To their great Father, prayers were offer'd up,
Or praises for our Country's Victories,
And 'mid the simple worshippers, perchance,
I only, like an uninvited Guest
Whom no one own'd sate silent, shall I add,
Fed on the day of vengeance yet to come?
. . . .

After what hath been
Already said of patriotic love,
And hinted at in other sentiments
We need not linger long upon this theme.
This only may be said, that from the first
Having two natures in me, joy the one
The other melancholy, and withal
A happy man, and therefore bold to look
On painful things, slow, somewhat, too, and stern
In temperament, I took the knife in hand
And stopping not at parts less sensitive,
Endeavoured with my best of skill to probe
The living body of society
Even to the heart; I push'd without remorse
My speculations forward; yea, set foot
On Nature's holiest places. Time may come
When some dramatic Story may afford
Shapes livelier to convey to thee, my Friend,
What then I learn'd, or think I learn'd, of truth,
And the errors into which I was betray'd
By present objects, and by reasonings false
From the beginning, inasmuch as drawn
Out of a heart which had been turn'd aside
From Nature by external accidents,
And which was thus confounded more and more,
Misguiding and misguided. Thus I fared,
Dragging all passions, notions, shapes of faith,
Like culprits to the bar, suspiciously
Calling the mind to establish in plain day
Her titles and her honours, now believing,
Now disbelieving, endlessly perplex'd
With impulse, motive, right and wrong, the ground
Of moral obligation, what the rule

And what the sanction, till, demanding *proof,*
And seeking it in everything, I lost
All feeling of conviction, and, in fine,
Sick, wearied out with contrarieties,
Yielded up moral questions in despair,
And for my future studies, as the sole
Employment of the enquiring faculty,
Turn'd towards mathematics, and their clear
And solid evidence—Ah! then it was
That Thou, most precious Friend! about this time
First known to me, didst lend a living help
To regulate my Soul, and then it was
That the belovèd Woman in whose sight
Those days were pass'd, now speaking in a voice
Of sudden admonition, like a brook
That does but cross a lonely road, and now
Seen, heard and felt, and caught at every turn,
Companion never lost through many a league,
Maintain'd for me a saving intercourse
With my true self; for, though impair'd and chang'd
Much, as it seemed, I was no further chang'd
Than as a clouded, not a waning moon:
She, in the midst of all, preserv'd me still
A Poet, made me seek beneath that name
My office upon earth, and nowhere else,
And lastly, Nature's Self, by human love
Assisted, through the weary labyrinth
Conducted me again to open day,
Revived the feelings of my earlier life,
Gave me that strength and knowledge full of peace,
Enlarged, and never more to be disturb'd,
Which through the steps of our degeneracy,
All degradation of this age, hath still
Upheld me, and upholds me at this day

In the catastrophe (for so they dream,
And nothing less), when finally, to close
And rivet up the gains of France, a Pope
Is summon'd in to crown an Emperor;
This last opprobrium, when we see the dog
Returning to his vomit, when the sun
That rose in splendour, was alive, and moved
In exultation among living clouds
Hath put his function and his glory off,
And, turned into a gewgaw, a machine,
Sets like an opera phantom.

BOOK THIRTEENTH

CONCLUSION

. . . .
In one of these excursions, travelling then
Through Wales on foot, and with a youthful Friend,
I left Bethkelet's huts at couching-time,
And westward took my way to see the sun
Rise from the top of Snowdon. Having reach'd
The Cottage at the Mountain's foot, we there
Rouz'd up the Shepherd, who by ancient right
Of office is the Stranger's usual guide;
And after short refreshment sallied forth.

    It was a Summer's night, a close warm night,
Wan, dull and glaring, with a dripping mist
Low-hung and thick that cover'd all the sky,
Half threatening storm and rain; but on we went
Uncheck'd, being full of heart and having faith
In our tried Pilot. Little could we see
Hemm'd round on every side with fog and damp,

And, after ordinary travellers' chat
With our Conductor, silently we sank
Each into commerce with his private thoughts:
Thus did we breast the ascent, and by myself
Was nothing either seen or heard the while
Which took me from my musings, save that once
The Shepherd's Cur did to his own great joy
Unearth a hedgehog in the mountain crags
Round which he made a barking turbulent.
This small adventure, for even such it seemed
In that wild place and at the dead of night,
Being over and forgotten, on we wound
In silence as before. With forehead bent
Earthward, as if in opposition set
Against an enemy, I panted up
With eager pace, and no less eager thoughts.
Thus might we wear perhaps an hour away,
Ascending at loose distance each from each,
And I, as chanced, the foremost of the Band;
When at my feet the ground appear'd to brighten,
And with a step or two seem'd brighter still;
Nor had I time to ask the cause of this,
For instantly a Light upon the turf
Fell like a flash: I looked about, and lo!
The Moon stood naked in the Heavens, at height
Immense above my head, and on the shore
I found myself of a huge sea of mist,
Which, meek and silent, rested at my feet:
A hundred hills their dusky backs upheaved
All over this still Ocean, and beyond,
Far, far beyond, the vapours shot themselves,
In headlands, tongues, and promontory shapes,
Into the Sea, the real Sea, that seem'd
To dwindle, and give up its majesty,

Usurp'd upon as far as sight could reach.
Meanwhile, the Moon look'd down upon this shew
In single glory, and we stood, the mist
Touching our very feet; and from the shore
At distance not the third part of a mile
Was a blue chasm; a fracture in the vapour,
A deep and gloomy breathing-place through which
Mounted the roar of waters, torrents, streams
Innumerable, roaring with one voice.
The universal spectacle throughout
Was shaped for admiration and delight,
Grand in itself alone, but in that breach
Through which the homeless voice of waters rose,
That dark deep thoroughfare had Nature lodg'd
The Soul, the Imagination of the whole.

    A meditation rose in me that night
Upon the lonely Mountain when the scene
Had pass'd away, and it appear'd to me
The perfect image of a mighty Mind,
Of one that feeds upon infinity,
That is exalted by an underpresence,
The sense of God, or whatsoe'er is dim
Or vast in its own being, above all
One function of such mind had Nature there
Exhibited by putting forth, and that
With circumstance most awful and sublime,
That domination which she oftentimes
Exerts upon the outward face of things,
So moulds them, and endues, abstracts, combines,
Or by abrupt and unhabitual influence
Doth make one object so impress itself
Upon all others, and pervade them so
That even the grossest minds must see and hear

And cannot chuse but feel. The Power which these
Acknowledge when thus moved, which Nature thus
Thrusts forth upon the senses, is the express
Resemblance, in the fulness of its strength
Made visible, a genuine Counterpart
And Brother of the glorious faculty
Which higher minds bear with them as their own.
That is the very spirit in which they deal
With all the objects of the universe;
They from their native selves can send abroad
Like transformations, for themselves create
A like existence, and, whene'er it is
Created for them, catch it by an instinct;
Them the enduring and the transient both
Serve to exalt; they build up greatest things
From least suggestions, ever on the watch,
Willing to work and to be wrought upon,
They need not extraordinary calls
To rouze them, in a world of life they live,
By sensible impressions not enthrall'd,
But quicken'd, rouz'd, and made thereby more fit
To hold communion with the invisible world.
Such minds are truly from the Deity,
For they are Powers; and hence the highest bliss
That can be known is theirs, the consciousness
Of whom they are habitually infused
Through every image, and through every thought,
And all impressions; hence religion, faith,
And endless occupation for the soul
Whether discursive or intuitive;
Hence sovereignty within and peace at will
Emotion which best foresight need not fear
Most worthy then of trust when most intense.
Hence chearfulness in every act of life

Hence truth in moral judgements and delight
That fails not in the external universe.
. . . .

I travelled among unknown men

I travelled among unknown men,
   In lands beyond the sea;
Nor, England! did I know till then
   What love I bore to thee.

'Tis past, that melancholy dream!
   Nor will I quit thy shore
A second time; for still I seem
   To love thee more and more.

Among thy mountains did I feel
   The joy of my desire;
And she I cherished turned her wheel
   Beside an English fire.

Thy mornings showed, thy nights concealed,
   The bowers where Lucy played;
And thine too is the last green field
   That Lucy's eyes surveyed.

To the Cuckoo

O blithe New-comer! I have heard,
I hear thee and rejoice.
O Cuckoo! shall I call thee Bird,
Or but a wandering Voice?

While I am lying on the grass
Thy twofold shout I hear,
From hill to hill it seems to pass,
At once far off, and near.

Though babbling only to the Vale,
Of sunshine and of flowers,
Thou bringest unto me a tale
Of visionary hours.

Thrice welcome, darling of the Spring!
Even yet thou art to me
No bird, but an invisible thing,
A voice, a mystery;

The same whom in my schoolboy days
I listened to; that Cry
Which made me look a thousand ways
In bush, and tree, and sky.

To seek thee did I often rove
Through woods and on the green;
And thou wert still a hope, a love;
Still longed for, never seen.

And I can listen to thee yet;
Can lie upon the plain
And listen, till I do beget
That golden time again.

O blessèd Bird! the earth we pace
Again appears to be
An unsubstantial, faery place;
That is fit home for Thee!

My heart leaps up when I behold

My heart leaps up when I behold
    A rainbow in the sky:
So was it when my life began;
So is it now I am a man;
So be it when I shall grow old,
    Or let me die!
The Child is father of the Man;
And I could wish my days to be
Bound each to each by natural piety.

Ode

INTIMATIONS OF IMMORTALITY FROM
RECOLLECTIONS OF EARLY CHILDHOOD

The Child is Father of the Man;
And I could wish my days to be
Bound each to each by natural piety.

I

There was a time when meadow, grove, and stream,
The earth, and every common sight,
    To me did seem
    Apparelled in celestial light,
The glory and the freshness of a dream.
It is not now as it hath been of yore;—
    Turn whereso'er I may,
      By night or day,
The things which I have seen I now can see no more.

II

The Rainbow comes and goes,
  And lovely is the Rose;
  The Moon doth with delight
Look round her when the heavens are bare;
    Waters on a starry night
    Are beautiful and fair;
  The sunshine is a glorious birth;
  But yet I know, where'er I go,
That there hath past away a glory from the earth.

III

Now, while the birds thus sing a joyous song,
  And while the young lambs bound
    As to the tabor's sound,
To me alone there came a thought of grief:
A timely utterance gave that thought relief,
    And I again am strong:
The cataracts blow their trumpets from the steep;
No more shall grief of mine the season wrong;
I hear the Echoes through the mountains throng,
The Winds come to me from the fields of sleep,
    And all the earth is gay;
      Land and sea
    Give themselves up to jollity,
      And with the heart of May
    Doth every Beast keep holiday;—
      Thou Child of Joy,
Shout round me, let me hear thy shouts, thou happy
      Shepherd-boy!

IV

Ye blessèd Creatures, I have heard the call
  Ye to each other make; I see
The heavens laugh with you in your jubilee;

My heart is at your festival,
    My head hath its coronal,
The fulness of your bliss, I feel—I feel it all.
    Oh evil day! if I were sullen
    While Earth herself is adorning,
      This sweet May-morning,
    And the Children are culling
      On every side,
    In a thousand valleys far and wide,
    Fresh flowers; while the sun shines warm,
And the Babe leaps up on his Mother's arm:—
    I hear, I hear, with joy I hear!
    —But there's a Tree, of many, one,
A single Field which I have looked upon,
Both of them speak of something that is gone:
    The Pansy at my feet
    Doth the same tale repeat:
Whither is fled the visionary gleam?
Where is it now, the glory and the dream?

          V
Our birth is but a sleep and a forgetting:
The Soul that rises with us, our life's Star,
    Hath had elsewhere its setting,
      And cometh from afar:
    Not in entire forgetfulness,
    And not in utter nakedness,
But trailing clouds of glory do we come
    From God, who is our home:
Heaven lies about us in our infancy!
Shades of the prison-house begin to close
    Upon the growing Boy,
      But He
Beholds the light, and whence it flows,
    He sees it in his joy;

The Youth, who daily farther from the east
    Must travel, still is Nature's Priest,
    And by the vision splendid
    Is on his way attended;
At length the Man perceives it die away,
And fade into the light of common day.

VI

Earth fills her lap with pleasures of her own;
Yearnings she hath in her own natural kind,
And, even with something of a Mother's mind,
    And no unworthy aim,
    The homely Nurse doth all she can
To make her Foster-child, her Inmate Man,
    Forget the glories he hath known,
And that imperial palace whence he came.

VII

Behold the Child among his new-born blisses,
A six years' Darling of a pigmy size!
See, where 'mid work of his own hand he lies,
Fretted by sallies of his mother's kisses,
With light upon him from his father's eyes!
See, at his feet, some little plan or chart,
Some fragment from his dream of human life,
Shaped by himself with newly-learnèd art;
    A wedding or a festival,
    A mourning or a funeral;
      And this hath now his heart,
    And unto this he frames his song:
      Then will he fit his tongue
To dialogues of business, love, or strife;
    But it will not be long

Ere this be thrown aside,
And with new joy and pride
The little Actor cons another part;
Filling from time to time his 'humorous stage'
With all the Persons, down to palsied Age,
That Life brings with her in her equipage;
As if his whole vocation
Were endless imitation.

VIII

Thou, whose exterior semblance doth belie
Thy Soul's immensity;
Thou best Philosopher, who yet dost keep
Thy heritage, thou Eye among the blind,
That, deaf and silent, read'st the eternal deep,
Haunted for ever by the eternal mind,—
Mighty Prophet! Seer blest!
On whom those truths do rest,
Which we are toiling all our lives to find,
In darkness lost, the darkness of the grave;
Thou, over whom thy Immortality
Broods like the Day, a Master o'er a Slave,
A Presence which is not to be put by;
Thou little Child, yet glorious in the might
Of heaven-born freedom on thy being's height,
Why with such earnest pains dost thou provoke
The years to bring the inevitable yoke,
Thus blindly with thy blessedness at strife?
Full soon thy Soul shall have her earthly freight,
And custom lie upon thee with a weight,
Heavy as frost, and deep almost as life!

IX

O joy! that in our embers
Is something that doth live,
That nature yet remembers
What was so fugitive!
The thought of our past years in me doth breed
Perpetual benediction: not indeed
For that which is most worthy to be blest;
Delight and liberty, the simple creed
Of Childhood, whether busy or at rest,
With new-fledged hope still fluttering in his breast:—
      Not for these I raise
      The song of thanks and praise;
   But for those obstinate questionings
   Of sense and outward things,
   Fallings from us, vanishings;
   Blank misgivings of a Creature
Moving about in worlds not realized,
High instincts before which our mortal Nature
Did tremble like a guilty Thing surprised:
      But for those first affections,
      Those shadowy recollections,
   Which, be they what they may,
Are yet the fountain light of all our day,
Are yet a master light of all our seeing;
   Uphold us, cherish, and have power to make
Our noisy years seem moments in the being
Of the eternal Silence: truths that wake,
      To perish never;
Which neither listlessness, nor mad endeavour,
      Nor Man nor Boy,
Nor all that is at enmity with joy,
Can utterly abolish or destroy!

Hence in a season of calm weather
    Though inland far we be,
Our Souls have sight of that immortal sea
    Which brought us hither,
  Can in a moment travel thither,
And see the Children sport upon the shore,
And hear the mighty waters rolling evermore.

X

Then sing, ye Birds, sing, sing a joyous song!
    And let the young Lambs bound
    As to the tabor's sound!
We in thought will join your throng,
    Ye that pipe and ye that play,
    Ye that through your hearts today
    Feel the gladness of the May!
What though the radiance which was once so bright
Be now for ever taken from my sight,
    Though nothing can bring back the hour
Of splendour in the grass, of glory in the flower;
    We will grieve not, rather find
    Strength in what remains behind;
    In the primal sympathy
    Which having been must ever be;
    In the soothing thoughts that spring
    Out of human suffering;
    In the faith that looks through death,
In years that bring the philosophic mind.

XI

And O, ye Fountains, Meadows, Hills, and Groves,
Forebode not any severing of our loves!

Yet in my heart of hearts I feel your might;
I only have relinquished one delight
To live beneath your more habitual sway.
I love the Brooks which down their channels fret,
Even more than when I tripped lightly as they;
The innocent brightness of a new-born Day
      Is lovely yet;
The Clouds that gather round the setting sun
Do take a sober colouring from an eye
That hath kept watch o'er man's mortality;
Another race hath been, and other palms are won.
Thanks to the human heart by which we live,
Thanks to its tenderness, its joys, and fears,
To me the meanest flower that blows can give
Thoughts that do often lie too deep for tears.

Resolution and Independence

I

There was a roaring in the wind all night;
The rain came heavily and fell in floods;
But now the sun is rising calm and bright;
The birds are singing in the distant woods;
Over his own sweet voice the Stock-dove broods;
The Jay makes answer as the Magpie chatters;
And all the air is filled with pleasant noise of waters.

II

All things that love the sun are out of doors;
The sky rejoices in the morning's birth;
The grass is bright with rain-drops;—on the moors
The hare is running races in her mirth;
And with her feet she from the plashy earth

Raises a mist; that, glittering in the sun,
Runs with her all the way, wherever she doth run.

III

I was a Traveller then upon the moor;
I saw the hare that raced about with joy;
I heard the woods and distant waters roar;
Or heard them not, as happy as a boy:
The pleasant season did my heart employ:
My old remembrances went from me wholly;
And all the ways of men, so vain and melancholy.

IV

But, as it sometimes chanceth, from the might
Of joy in minds that can no further go,
As high as we have mounted in delight
In our dejection do we sink as low;
To me that morning did it happen so;
And fears and fancies thick upon me came;
Dim sadness—and blind thoughts, I knew not, nor could name.

V

I heard the sky-lark warbling in the sky;
And I bethought me of the playful hare:
Even such a happy Child of earth am I;
Even as these blissful creatures do I fare;
Far from the world I walk, and from all care;
But there may come another day to me—
Solitude, pain of heart, distress, and poverty.

VI

My whole life I have lived in pleasant thought,
As if life's business were a summer mood;
As if all needful things would come unsought

To genial faith, still rich in genial good;
But how can He expect that others should
Build for him, sow for him, and at his call
Love him, who for himself will take no heed at all?

VII

I thought of Chatterton, the marvellous Boy,
The sleepless Soul that perished in his pride;
Of Him who walked in glory and in joy
Following his plough, along the mountain-side:
By our own spirits are we deified:
We Poets in our youth begin in gladness;
But thereof come in the end despondency and madness.

VIII

Now, whether it were by peculiar grace,
A leading from above, a something given,
Yet it befell, that, in this lonely place,
When I with these untoward thoughts had striven,
Beside a pool bare to the eye of heaven
I saw a Man before me unawares:
The oldest man he seemed that ever wore grey hairs.

IX

As a huge stone is sometimes seen to lie
Couched on the bald top of an eminence;
Wonder to all who do the same espy,
By what means it could thither come, and whence;
So that it seems a thing endued with sense:
Like a sea-beast crawled forth, that on a shelf
Of rock or sand reposeth, there to sun itself;

X

Such seemed this Man, not all alive nor dead,
Nor all asleep—in his extreme old age:
His body was bent double, feet and head
Coming together in life's pilgrimage;
As if some dire constraint of pain, or rage
Of sickness felt by him in times long past,
A more than human weight upon his frame had cast.

XI

Himself he propped, limbs, body, and pale face,
Upon a long grey staff of shaven wood:
And, still as I drew near with gentle pace,
Upon the margin of that moorish flood
Motionless as a cloud the old Man stood,
That heareth not the loud winds when they call;
And moveth all together, if it move at all.

XII

At length, himself unsettling, he the pond
Stirred with his staff, and fixedly did look
Upon the muddy water, which he conned,
As if he had been reading in a book:
And now a stranger's privilege I took;
And, drawing to his side, to him did say,
'This morning gives us promise of a glorious day.'

XIII

A gentle answer did the old Man make,
In courteous speech which forth he slowly drew:
And him with further words I thus bespake,
'What occupation do you there pursue?
This is a lonesome place for one like you.'

Ere he replied, a flash of mild surprise
Broke from the sable orbs of his yet-vivid eyes.

XIV

His words came feebly, from a feeble chest,
But each in solemn order followed each,
With something of a lofty utterance drest—
Choice word and measured phrase, above the reach
Of ordinary men; a stately speech;
Such as grave Livers do in Scotland use,
Religious men, who give to God and man their dues.

XV

He told, that to these waters he had come
To gather leeches, being old and poor:
Employment hazardous and wearisome!
And he had many hardships to endure:
From pond to pond he roamed, from moor to moor;
Housing, with God's good help, by choice or chance;
And in this way he gained an honest maintenance.

XVI

The old Man still stood talking by my side;
But now his voice to me was like a stream
Scarce heard; nor word from word could I divide;
And the whole body of the Man did seem
Like one whom I had met with in a dream;
Or like a man from some far region sent,
To give me human strength, by apt admonishment.

XVII

My former thoughts returned: the fear that kills;
And hope that is unwilling to be fed;
Cold, pain, and labour, and all fleshly ills;

And mighty Poets in their misery dead.
—Perplexed, and longing to be comforted,
My question eagerly did I renew,
'How is it that you live, and what is it you do?'

XVIII
He with a smile did then his words repeat;
And said that, gathering leeches, far and wide
He travelled; stirring thus about his feet
The waters of the pools where they abide.
'Once I could meet with them on every side;
But they have dwindled long by slow decay;
Yet still I persevere, and find them where I may.'

XIX
While he was talking thus, the lonely place,
The old Man's shape, and speech—all troubled me:
In my mind's eye I seemed to see him pace
About the weary moors continually,
Wandering about alone and silently.
While I these thoughts within myself pursued,
He, having made a pause, the same discourse renewed.

XX
And soon with this he other matter blended,
Cheerfully uttered, with demeanour kind,
But stately in the main; and when he ended,
I could have laughed myself to scorn to find
In that decrepit Man so firm a mind.
'God,' said I, 'be my help and stay secure;
I'll think of the Leech-gatherer on the lonely moor!'

Travelling

This is the spot:—how mildly does the sun
Shine in between the fading leaves! the air
In the habitual silence of this wood
Is more than silent; and this bed of heath—
Where shall we find so sweet a resting-place?
Come, let me see thee sink into a dream
Of quiet thoughts, protracted till thine eye
Be calm as water when the winds are gone
And no one can tell whither. My sweet Friend,
We two have had such happy hours together
That my heart melts in me to think of it.

1801

I grieved for Buonaparté, with a vain
And an unthinking grief! The tenderest mood
Of that Man's mind—what can it be? what food
Fed his first hopes? what knowledge could *he* gain?
'Tis not in battles that from youth we train
The Governor who must be wise and good,
And temper with the sternness of the brain
Thoughts motherly, and meek as womanhood.
Wisdom doth live with children round her knees:
Books, leisure, perfect freedom, and the talk
Man holds with week-day man in the hourly walk
Of the mind's business: these are the degrees
By which true Sway doth mount; this is the stalk
True Power doth grow on; and her rights are these.

Great men have been among us; hands that penned

Great men have been among us; hands that penned
And tongues that uttered wisdom—better none:
The later Sidney, Marvell, Harrington,
Young Vane, and others who called Milton friend.
These moralists could act and comprehend:
They knew how genuine glory was put on;
Taught us how rightfully a nation shone
In splendour: what strength was, that would not bend
But in magnanimous meekness. France, 'tis strange,
Hath brought forth no such souls as we had then.
Perpetual emptiness! unceasing change!
No single volume paramount, no code,
No master spirit, no determined road;
But equally a want of books and men!

Personal Talk

I

I am not One who much or oft delight
To season my fireside with personal talk,—
Of friends, who live within an easy walk,
Or neighbours, daily, weekly, in my sight:
And, for my chance-acquaintance, ladies bright,
Sons, mothers, maidens withering on the stalk,
These all wear out of me, like Forms, with chalk
Painted on rich men's floors, for one feast-night.
Better than such discourse doth silence long,
Long, barren silence, square with my desire;
To sit without emotion, hope, or aim,
In the loved presence of my cottage-fire,
And listen to the flapping of the flame,
Or kettle whispering its faint undersong.

The world is too much with us; late and soon

The world is too much with us; late and soon,
Getting and spending, we lay waste our powers:
Little we see in Nature that is ours;
We have given our hearts away, a sordid boon!
This Sea that bares her bosom to the moon;
The winds that will be howling at all hours,
And are up-gathered now like sleeping flowers;
For this, for everything, we are out of tune;
It moves us not.—Great God! I'd rather be
A Pagan suckled in a creed outworn;
So might I, standing on this pleasant lea,
Have glimpses that would make me less forlorn;
Have sight of Proteus rising from the sea;
Or hear old Triton blow his wreathèd horn.

To the Memory of Raisley Calvert

Calvert! it must not be unheard by them
Who may respect my name, that I to thee
Owed many years of early liberty.
This care was thine when sickness did condemn
Thy youth to hopeless wasting, root and stem—
That I, if frugal and severe, might stray
Where'er I liked; and finally array
My temples with the Muse's diadem.
Hence, if in freedom I have loved the truth;
If there be aught of pure, or good, or great,
In my past verse; or shall be, in the lays
Of higher mood, which now I meditate;—
It gladdens me, O worthy, short-lived, Youth!
To think how much of this will be thy praise.

With Ships the sea was sprinkled far and nigh

With Ships the sea was sprinkled far and nigh,
Like stars in heaven, and joyously it showed;
Some lying fast at anchor in the road,
Some veering up and down, one knew not why.
A goodly Vessel did I then espy
Come like a giant from a haven broad;
And lustily along the bay she strode,
Her tackling rich, and of apparel high.
This Ship was naught to me, nor I to her,
Yet I pursued her with a Lover's look;
This Ship to all the rest did I prefer:
When will she turn, and whither? She will brook
No tarrying; where She comes the winds must stir:
On went She, and due north her journey took.

Composed Upon Westminster Bridge, September 3, 1802

Earth has not anything to show more fair:
Dull would he be of soul who could pass by
A sight so touching in its majesty:
This City now doth, like a garment, wear
The beauty of the morning; silent, bare,
Ships, towers, domes, theatres, and temples lie
Open unto the fields, and to the sky;
All bright and glittering in the smokeless air.
Never did sun more beautifully steep
In his first splendour, valley, rock, or hill;
Ne'er saw I, never felt, a calm so deep!
The river glideth at his own sweet will:
Dear God! the very houses seem asleep;
And all that mighty heart is lying still!

Composed near Calais, on the Road
Leading to Ardres, August 7, 1802

Jones! as from Calais southward you and I
Went pacing side by side, this public Way
Streamed with the pomp of a too-credulous day,
When faith was pledged to new-born Liberty:
A homeless sound of joy was in the sky:
From hour to hour the antiquated Earth
Beat like the heart of Man: songs, garlands, mirth,
Banners, and happy faces, far and nigh!
And now, sole register that these things were,
Two solitary greetings have I heard,
'Good morrow, Citizen!' a hollow word,
As if a dead man spake it! Yet despair
Touches me not, though pensive as a bird
Whose vernal coverts winter hath laid bare.

It is a beauteous evening, calm and free

It is a beauteous evening, calm and free,
The holy time is quiet as a Nun
Breathless with adoration; the broad sun
Is sinking down in its tranquillity;
The gentleness of heaven broods o'er the Sea:
Listen! the mighty Being is awake,
And doth with his eternal motion make
A sound like thunder—everlastingly.
Dear Child! dear Girl! that walkest with me here,
If thou appear untouched by solemn thought,
Thy nature is not therefore less divine:
Thou liest in Abraham's bosom all the year;

And worshipp'st at the Temple's inner shrine,
God being with thee when we know it not.

To Toussaint l'Ouverture

Toussaint, the most unhappy man of men!
Whether the whistling Rustic tend his plough
Within thy hearing, or thy head be now
Pillowed in some deep dungeon's earless den;—
O miserable Chieftain! where and when
Wilt thou find patience! Yet die not; do thou
Wear rather in thy bonds a cheerful brow:
Though fallen thyself, never to rise again,
Live, and take comfort. Thou hast left behind
Powers that will work for thee; air, earth, and skies;
There's not a breathing of the common wind
That will forget thee; thou hast great allies;
Thy friends are exultations, agonies,
And love, and man's unconquerable mind.

Calais, August 15, 1802

Festivals have I seen that were not names:
This is young Buonaparté's natal day,
And his is henceforth an established sway—
Consul for life. With worship France proclaims
Her approbation, and with pomps and games.
Heaven grant that other Cities may be gay!
Calais is not: and I have bent my way
To the sea-coast, noting that each man frames
His business as he likes. Far other show
My youth here witnessed, in a prouder time;

The senselessness of joy was then sublime!
Happy is he, who, caring not for Pope,
Consul, or King, can sound himself to know
The destiny of Man, and live in hope.

September, 1802. Near Dover

Inland, within a hollow vale, I stood;
And saw, while sea was calm and air was clear,
The coast of France—the coast of France how near!
Drawn almost into frightful neighbourhood.
I shrunk; for verily the barrier flood
Was like a lake, or river bright and fair,
A span of waters; yet what power is there!
What mightiness for evil and for good!
Even so doth God protect us if we be
Virtuous and wise. Winds blow, and waters roll,
Strength to the brave, and Power, and Deity;
Yet in themselves are nothing! One decree
Spake laws to *them,* and said that by the soul
Only, the Nations shall be great and free.

London, 1802

Milton! thou shouldst be living at this hour:
England hath need of thee: she is a fen
Of stagnant waters: altar, sword, and pen,
Fireside, the heroic wealth of hall and bower,
Have forfeited their ancient English dower
Of inward happiness. We are selfish men;
Oh! raise us up, return to us again;
And give us manners, virtue, freedom, power.

Thy soul was like a Star, and dwelt apart:
Thou hadst a voice whose sound was like the sea:
Pure as the naked heavens, majestic, free,
So didst thou travel on life's common way,
In cheerful godliness; and yet thy heart
The lowliest duties on herself did lay.

Written in London, September, 1802

O Friend! I know not which way I must look
For comfort, being, as I am, opprest,
To think that now our life is only drest
For show; mean handy-work of craftsman, cook,
Or groom!—We must run glittering like a brook
In the open sunshine, or we are unblest:
The wealthiest man among us is the best:
No grandeur now in nature or in book
Delights us. Rapine, avarice, expense,
This is idolatry; and these we adore:
Plain living and high thinking are no more:
The homely beauty of the good old cause
Is gone; our peace, our fearful innocence,
And pure religion breathing household laws.

October, 1803

When, looking on the present face of things,
I see one man, of men the meanest too!
Raised up to sway the world, to do, undo,
With mighty Nations for his underlings,
The great events with which old story rings
Seem vain and hollow; I find nothing great:

Nothing is left which I can venerate;
So that a doubt almost within me springs
Of Providence, such emptiness at length
Seems at the heart of all things. But, great God!
I measure back the steps which I have trod;
And tremble, seeing whence proceeds the strength
Of such poor Instruments, with thoughts sublime
I tremble at the sorrow of the time.

Yarrow Unvisited

See the various Poems the scene of which is laid upon the banks of the Yarrow;
in particular, the exquisite Ballad of Hamilton beginning
'Busk ye, busk ye, my bonny, bonny Bride,
Busk ye, busk ye, my winsome Marrow!'—

From Stirling castle we had seen
The mazy Forth unravelled;
Had trod the banks of Clyde, and Tay,
And with the Tweed had travelled;
And when we came to Clovenford,
Then said my *'winsome Marrow,'*
'Whate'er betide, we'll turn aside,
And see the Braes of Yarrow.'

'Let Yarrow folk, *frae* Selkirk town,
Who have been buying, selling,
Go back to Yarrow, 'tis their own;
Each maiden to her dwelling!
On Yarrow's banks let herons feed,
Hares couch, and rabbits burrow!
But we will downward with the Tweed,
Nor turn aside to Yarrow.

'There's Galla Water, Leader Haughs,
Both lying right before us;
And Dryborough, where with chiming Tweed
The lintwhites sing in chorus;
There's pleasant Tiviot-dale, a land
Made blithe with plough and harrow:
Why throw away a needful day
To go in search of Yarrow?

'What's Yarrow but a river bare,
That glides the dark hills under?
There are a thousand such elsewhere
As worthy of your wonder.'
—Strange words they seemed of slight and scorn;
My True-love sighed for sorrow;
And looked me in the face, to think
I thus could speak of Yarrow!

'Oh! green,' said I, 'are Yarrow's holms,
And sweet is Yarrow flowing!
Fair hangs the apple frae the rock,
But we will leave it growing.
O'er hilly path, and open Strath,
We'll wander Scotland thorough;
But, though so near, we will not turn
Into the dale of Yarrow.

'Let beeves and home-bred kine partake
The sweets of Burn-mill meadow;
The swan on still St Mary's Lake
Float double, swan and shadow!
We will not see them; will not go,
Today, nor yet tomorrow;

Enough if in our hearts we know
There's such a place as Yarrow.

'Be Yarrow stream unseen, unknown!
It must, or we shall rue it:
We have a vision of our own;
Ah! why should we undo it?
The treasured dreams of times long past,
We'll keep them, winsome Marrow!
For when we're there, although 'tis fair,
'Twill be another Yarrow!

'If Care with freezing years should come,
And wandering seem but folly,—
Should we be loth to stir from home,
And yet be melancholy;
Should life be dull, and spirits low,
'Twill soothe us in our sorrow,
That earth hath something yet to show,
The bonny holms of Yarrow!'

The Small Celandine

There is a Flower, the lesser Celandine,
That shrinks, like many more, from cold and rain;
And, the first moment that the sun may shine,
Bright as the sun himself, 'tis out again!

When hailstones have been falling, swarm on swarm,
Or blasts the green field and the trees distrest,
Oft have I seen it muffled up from harm,
In close self-shelter, like a Thing at rest.

But lately, one rough day, this Flower I passed
And recognized it, though an altered form,
Now standing forth an offering to the blast,
And buffeted at will by rain and storm.

I stopped, and said with inly-muttered voice,
'It doth not love the shower, nor seek the cold:
This neither is its courage nor its choice,
But its necessity in being old.

'The sunshine may not cheer it, nor the dew;
It cannot help itself in its decay;
Stiff in its members, withered, changed of hue.'
And, in my spleen, I smiled that it was grey.

To be a Prodigal's Favourite—then, worse truth,
A Miser's Pensioner—behold our lot!
O Man, that from thy fair and shining youth
Age might but take the things Youth needed not!

I wandered lonely as a cloud

I wandered lonely as a cloud
That floats on high o'er vales and hills,
When all at once I saw a crowd,
A host, of golden daffodils;
Beside the lake, beneath the trees,
Fluttering and dancing in the breeze.

Continuous as the stars that shine
And twinkle on the milky way,
They stretched in never-ending line
Along the margin of a bay:

Ten thousand saw I at a glance,
Tossing their heads in sprightly dance.

The waves beside them danced; but they
Out-did the sparkling waves in glee:
A poet could not but be gay,
In such a jocund company:
I gazed—and gazed—but little thought
What wealth the show to me had brought:

For oft, when on my couch I lie
In vacant or in pensive mood,
They flash upon that inward eye
Which is the bliss of solitude;
And then my heart with pleasure fills,
And dances with the daffodils.

*French Revolution As It Appeared
to Enthusiasts at Its Commencement*

REPRINTED FROM 'THE FRIEND'

Oh! pleasant exercise of hope and joy!
For mighty were the auxiliars which then stood
Upon our side, we who were strong in love!
Bliss was it in that dawn to be alive,
But to be young was very heaven!—Oh! times,
In which the meagre, stale, forbidding ways
Of custom, law, and statute, took at once
The attraction of a country in romance!
When Reason seemed the most to assert her rights,
When most intent on making of herself
A prime Enchantress—to assist the work,

Which then was going forward in her name!
Not favoured spots alone, but the whole earth,
The beauty wore of promise, that which sets
(As at some moment might not be unfelt
Among the bowers of paradise itself)
The budding rose above the rose full blown.
What temper at the prospect did not wake
To happiness unthought of? The inert
Were roused, and lively natures rapt away!
They who had fed their childhood upon dreams,
The playfellows of fancy, who had made
All powers of swiftness, subtlety, and strength
Their ministers,—who in lordly wise had stirred
Among the grandest objects of the sense,
And dealt with whatsoever they found there
As if they had within some lurking right
To wield it;—they, too, who, of gentle mood,
Had watched all gentle motions, and to these
Had fitted their own thoughts, schemers more mild,
And in the region of their peaceful selves;—
Now was it that both found, the meek and lofty
Did both find, helpers to their heart's desire,
And stuff at hand, plastic as they could wish;
Were called upon to exercise their skill,
Not in Utopia, subterranean fields,
Or some secreted island, Heaven knows where!
But in the very world, which is the world
Of all of us,—the place where in the end
We find our happiness, or not at all!

The Simplon Pass

——Brook and road
Were fellow-travellers in this gloomy Pass,
And with them did we journey several hours
At a slow step. The immeasurable height
Of woods decaying, never to be decayed,
The stationary blasts of waterfalls,
And in the narrow rent, at every turn,
Winds thwarting winds bewildered and forlorn,
The torrents shooting from the clear blue sky,
The rocks that muttered close upon our ears,
Black drizzling crags that spake by the wayside
As if a voice were in them, the sick sight
And giddy prospect of the raving stream,
The unfettered clouds and region of the heavens,
Tumult and peace, the darkness and the light—
Were all like workings of one mind, the features
Of the same face, blossoms upon one tree,
Characters of the great Apocalypse,
The types and symbols of Eternity,
Of first, and last, and midst, and without end.

Elegiac Stanzas Suggested by a Picture of Peele Castle, in a Storm, Painted by Sir George Beaumont

I was thy neighbour once, thou rugged Pile!
Four summer weeks I dwelt in sight of thee:
I saw thee every day; and all the while
Thy Form was sleeping on a glassy sea.

So pure the sky, so quiet was the air!
So like, so very like, was day to day!

Whene'er I looked, thy Image still was there;
It trembled, but it never passed away.

How perfect was the calm! it seemed no sleep;
No mood, which season takes away, or brings:
I could have fancied that the mighty Deep
Was even the gentlest of all gentle Things.

Ah! THEN, if mine had been the Painter's hand,
To express what then I saw; and add the gleam,
The light that never was, on sea or land,
The consecration, and the Poet's dream;

I would have planted thee, thou hoary Pile
Amid a world how different from this!
Beside a sea that could not cease to smile;
On tranquil land, beneath a sky of bliss.

Thou shouldst have seemed a treasure-house divine
Of peaceful years; a chronicle of heaven;—
Of all the sunbeams that did ever shine
The very sweetest had to thee been given.

A Picture had it been of lasting ease,
Elysian quiet, without toil or strife;
No motion but the moving tide, a breeze,
Or merely silent Nature's breathing life.

Such, in the fond illusion of my heart,
Such Picture would I at that time have made:
And seen the soul of truth in every part,
A stedfast peace that might not be betrayed.

So once it would have been,—'tis so no more;
I have submitted to a new control:
A power is gone, which nothing can restore;
A deep distress hath humanized my Soul.

Not for a moment could I now behold
A smiling sea, and be what I have been:
The feeling of my loss will ne'er be old;
This, which I know, I speak with mind serene.

Then, Beaumont, Friend! who would have been the Friend,
If he had lived, of Him whom I deplore,
This work of thine I blame not, but commend;
This sea in anger, and that dismal shore.

O 'tis a passionate Work!—yet wise and well,
Well chosen is the spirit that is here;
That Hulk which labours in the deadly swell,
This rueful sky, this pageantry of fear!

And this huge Castle, standing here sublime,
I love to see the look with which it braves,
Cased in the unfeeling armour of old time,
The lightning, the fierce wind, and trampling waves.

Farewell, farewell the heart that lives alone,
Housed in a dream, at distance from the Kind!
Such happiness, wherever it be known,
Is to be pitied; for 'tis surely blind.

But welcome fortitude, and patient cheer,
And frequent sights of what is to be borne!
Such sights, or worse, as are before me here.—
Not without hope we suffer and we mourn.

Stepping Westward

While my Fellow-traveller and I were walking by the side of Loch Ketterine, one fine evening after sunset, in our road to a Hut where, in the course of our Tour, we had been hospitably entertained some weeks before, we met, in one of the loneliest parts of that solitary region, two well-dressed Women, one of whom said to us, by way of greeting, 'What, you are stepping westward?'

> *'What, you are stepping westward?'*—'Yea.'
> —'Twould be a *wildish* destiny,
> If we, who thus together roam
> In a strange Land, and far from home,
> Were in this place the guests of Chance:
> Yet who would stop, or fear to advance,
> Though home or shelter he had none,
> With such a sky to lead him on?
>
>
> The dewy ground was dark and cold;
> Behind, all gloomy to behold;
> And stepping westward seemed to be
> A kind of *heavenly* destiny:
> I liked the greeting; 'twas a sound
> Of something without place or bound;
> And seemed to give me spiritual right
> To travel through that region bright.
>
>
> The voice was soft, and she who spake
> Was walking by her native lake:
> The salutation had to me
> The very sound of courtesy:
> Its power was felt; and while my eye
> Was fixed upon the glowing Sky,

The echo of the voice enwrought
A human sweetness with the thought
Of travelling through the world that lay
Before me in my endless way.

The Solitary Reaper

Behold her, single in the field,
Yon solitary Highland Lass!
Reaping and singing by herself;
Stop here, or gently pass!
Alone she cuts and binds the grain,
And sings a melancholy strain;
O listen! for the Vale profound
Is overflowing with the sound.

No Nightingale did ever chaunt
More welcome notes to weary bands
Of travellers in some shady haunt,
Among Arabian sands:
A voice so thrilling ne'er was heard
In spring-time from the Cuckoo-bird,
Breaking the silence of the seas
Among the farthest Hebrides.

Will no one tell me what she sings?—
Perhaps the plaintive numbers flow
For old, unhappy, far-off things,
And battles long ago:
Or is it some more humble lay,
Familiar matter of today?
Some natural sorrow, loss, or pain,
That has been, and may be again?

Whate'er the theme, the Maiden sang
As if her song could have no ending;
I saw her singing at her work,
And o'er the sickle bending;—
I listened, motionless and still;
And, as I mounted up the hill,
The music in my heart I bore,
Long after it was heard no more.

Thought of a Briton on the Subjugation of Switzerland

Two Voices are there; one is of the sea,
One of the mountains; each a mighty Voice:
In both from age to age thou didst rejoice,
They were thy chosen music, Liberty!
There came a Tyrant, and with holy glee
Thou fought'st against him; but hast vainly striven:
Thou from thy Alpine holds at length art driven,
Where not a torrent murmurs heard by thee.
Of one deep bliss thine ear hath been bereft:
Then cleave, O cleave to that which still is left;
For, high-souled Maid, what sorrow would it be
That Mountain floods should thunder as before,
And Ocean bellow from his rocky shore,
And neither awful Voice be heard by thee!

Though narrow be that old Man's cares, and near

—'gives to airy nothing
A local habitation and a name.'

Though narrow be that old Man's cares, and near,
The poor old Man is greater than he seems:
For he hath waking empire, wide as dreams;
An ample sovereignty of eye and ear.
Rich are his walks with supernatural cheer;
The region of his inner spirit teems
With vital sounds and monitory gleams
Of high astonishment and pleasing fear.
He the seven birds hath seen, that never part,
Seen the SEVEN WHISTLERS in their nightly rounds,
And counted them: and oftentimes will start—
For overhead are sweeping GABRIEL'S HOUNDS,
Doomed, with their impious Lord, the flying Hart
To chase for ever, on aërial grounds!

Composed by the Side of Grasmere Lake

Clouds, lingering yet, extend in solid bars
Through the grey west; and lo! these waters, steeled
By breezeless air to smoothest polish, yield
A vivid repetition of the stars;
Jove, Venus, and the ruddy crest of Mars
Amid his fellows beauteously revealed
At happy distance from earth's groaning field,
Where ruthless mortals wage incessant wars.
Is it a mirror?—or the nether Sphere
Opening to view the abyss in which she feeds

Her own calm fires?—But list! a voice is near;
Great Pan himself low-whispering through the reeds,
'Be thankful, thou; for, if unholy deeds
Ravage the world, tranquillity is here!'

Surprised by joy—impatient as the Wind

Surprised by joy—impatient as the Wind
I turned to share the transport—Oh! with whom
But Thee, deep buried in the silent tomb,
That spot which no vicissitude can find?
Love, faithful love, recalled thee to my mind—
But how could I forget thee? Through what power,
Even for the least division of an hour,
Have I been so beguiled as to be blind
To my most grievous loss!—That thought's return
Was the worst pang that sorrow ever bore,
Save one, one only, when I stood forlorn,
Knowing my heart's best treasure was no more;
That neither present time, nor years unborn
Could to my sight that heavenly face restore.

Lines

Composed at Grasmere, during a walk one Evening, after a stormy day, the Author having just read in a Newspaper that the dissolution of Mr Fox was hourly expected.

Loud is the Vale! the Voice is up
With which she speaks when storms are gone,
A mighty unison of streams!
Of all her Voices, One!

Loud is the Vale;—this inland Depth
In peace is roaring like the Sea;
Yon star upon the mountain-top
Is listening quietly.

Sad was I, even to pain deprest,
Importunate and heavy load!
The Comforter hath found me here,
Upon this lonely road;

And many thousands now are sad—
Wait the fulfilment of their fear;
For he must die who is their stay,
Their glory disappear.

A Power is passing from the earth
To breathless Nature's dark abyss;
But when the great and good depart
What is it more than this—

That Man, who is from God sent forth,
Doth yet again to God return?—
Such ebb and flow must ever be,
Then wherefore should we mourn?

from *The River Duddon*

XXXIV AFTER-THOUGHT

I THOUGHT *of Thee, my partner and my guide,*
As being past away.—Vain sympathies!
For, backward, Duddon! as I cast my eyes,
I see what was, and is, and will abide;

Still glides the Stream, and shall for ever glide;
The Form remains, the Function never dies;
While we, the brave, the mighty, and the wise,
We Men, who in our morn of youth defied
The elements, must vanish;—be it so!
Enough, if something from our hands have power
To live, and act, and serve the future hour;
And if, as toward the silent tomb we go,
Through love, through hope, and faith's transcendent dower,
We feel that we are greater than we know.

Extempore Effusion upon the Death of James Hogg

When first, descending from the moorlands,
I saw the Stream of Yarrow glide
Along a bare and open valley,
The Ettrick Shepherd was my guide.

When last along its banks I wandered,
Through groves that had begun to shed
Their golden leaves upon the pathways,
My steps the Border-minstrel led.

The mighty Minstrel breathes no longer,
'Mid mouldering ruins low he lies;
And death upon the braes of Yarrow,
Has closed the Shepherd-poet's eyes:

Nor has the rolling year twice measured,
From sign to sign, its stedfast course,
Since every mortal power of Coleridge
Was frozen at its marvellous source;

The rapt One, of the godlike forehead,
The heaven-eyed creature sleeps in earth:
And Lamb, the frolic and the gentle,
Has vanished from his lonely hearth.

Like clouds that rake the mountain-summits,
Or waves that own no curbing hand,
How fast has brother followed brother,
From sunshine to the sunless land!

Yet I, whose lids from infant slumber
Were earlier raised, remain to hear
A timid voice, that asks in whispers,
'Who next will drop and disappear?'

Our haughty life is crowned with darkness,
Like London with its own black wreath,
On which with thee, O Crabbe! forth-looking,
I gazed from Hampstead's breezy heath.

As if but yesterday departed,
Thou too art gone before; but why,
O'er ripe fruit, seasonably gathered,
Should frail survivors heave a sigh?

Mourn rather for that holy Spirit,
Sweet as the spring, as ocean deep;
For Her who, ere her summer faded,
Has sunk into a breathless sleep.

No more of old romantic sorrows,
For slaughtered Youth or love-lorn Maid!
With sharper grief is Yarrow smitten,
And Ettrick mourns with her their Poet dead.

✸ ABOUT THE EDITOR ✸

Seamus Heaney was born in Northern Ireland in 1939. He is the author of seven books of poetry, two collections of critical essays, and a translation (from the Irish) of the medieval tale of Mad Sweeney. He has been a lecturer in English at Queen's University, Belfast, and Carysfort College in Dublin, and also has been a visiting professor at the University of California in Berkeley. At present he teaches for one semester each year at Harvard University but otherwise makes his home in Dublin where he lives with his wife and three children.